SUCCESSFUL
SENIORS

I0088612

GLOBAL
PUBLISHING
G R O U P

Global Publishing Group
Australia • New Zealand • Singapore • America • London

SUCCESSFUL SENIORS

How to Look and Feel Ageless, Create Wealth, and Be Unforgettable

MAE-ROSE O'CONNELL

First Edition 2023

National Library of Australia
Cataloguing-in-Publication entry:

Successful Seniors: How to Look and Feel Ageless, Create Wealth, and Be Unforgettable - Mae-Rose O'Connell

1st ed.
ISBN: 978-1-925370-79-9 (pbk.)

A catalogue record for this book is available from the National Library of Australia

Published by Global Publishing Group
PO Box 258, Banyo, QLD 4014 Australia
Email admin@globalpublishinggroup.com.au

For further information about orders:
Phone: +61 7 3267 0747

DEDICATION

I dedicate this book to you, Daisy Gamboa, for your tireless grand effort behind the scenes. I am in such awe of your patience and support. Through our projects together we have grown closer and share a passion for creativity and progress. Mostly we share a deep sense of the importance of family, love and respect. Sense of duty and compassion is your middle name.

You are the "Everyone" archetype representing connection, community and authenticity. You have the power to connect with others on a deep and meaningful level and inspire them towards their own authenticity. Thank you for spreading your love my way.

-o0o-

I dedicate this book to all my mentors and teachers, all who have helped me heal, encouraged me to learn and inspired me to teach. You separated me from my limiting beliefs and drew out the qualities and potential you saw within me.

-o0o-

My dedicated and loving friend Sammy, your love and trust gave me the confidence and the safety I needed to meet my true self. I am continually inspired and humbled by your courage, resilience and dedication.

-o0o-

Helen, your support and belief in every way is such a gift, your "Special Gift" stands alone.

-o0o-

www.MaeRoseMethods.com

———————————— o0o ————————————

ACKNOWLEDGEMENTS

Wholeheartedly I acknowledge books, as they have been my refuge since I was a child. I found solace in books and do so till this very day.

I am so grateful to my father for the antique bookshelves filled to the brim with educational material that I often turned to because of our family's geographical isolation in a country town.

My love for books and my desire to become an author was ignited when I read the following quotes:

"If you're serious about fast tracking your success, then you must become the expert. Experts write books…so become an author"

"Bringing your Value to the Marketplace Will Ensure Your Success"

"You become like the people you spend the most time with, so pay any price to be in the presence of Extraordinary People"

Darren J. Stephens

Thank you, Darren, for being one of those extraordinary people. Your mentorship and leadership have inspired me to become an author. I am more than grateful for your support and encouragement. You have set the bar high as a role model and as a person of integrity.

-o0o-

No one creates alone. This book would not be in your hands without the brilliance and expertise of the team at Global Publishing Group.

The moment you meet Andrew Carter, Global CEO, you start to thank him for things he has not done yet, as you know he will deliver.

Thank you, Andrew, for your unending support, your encouragement and forward thinking. Respectfully I hold you in high esteem for your keen eye for talent and laughing at my jokes. You have set a fine example for us to follow with your amazing leadership.

-o0o-

www.MaeRoseMethods.com

IT
ALL
DEPENDS
ON
HOW
YOU
LOOK
AT
IT

-o0o-

FOREWORD

Welcome, my friends, to the incredible journey of "Successful Seniors" - a guide that unlocks the secrets to looking and feeling ageless, creating wealth and becoming truly unforgettable. I am honoured to lend my voice to Mae-Rose's powerful message, for it is a subject very close to my heart.

In a world that often associates aging with decline, it is time for us to rewrite the narrative. We have seen individuals who defy the odds, those who refuse to settle for the limitations society imposes upon them. These remarkable souls have shown us that age is not a barrier, but a remarkable opportunity for transformation and achievement; Mae-Rose is a perfect example of just that.

Within these pages you will discover the strategies, mindsets, and habits of those who have tapped into their ageless power. Mae-Rose delves into the secrets of physical vitality, revealing how to cultivate boundless energy and preserve the youthful vigour that resides within us all. She explores the art of wealth creation, sharing insights on how to maximise financial resources and leave a lasting legacy. Perhaps, most importantly, she uncovers the essence of being unforgettable, how to touch the lives of others and create a profound impact that resonates across generations.

"Successful Seniors" is not just a guide; it is a call to action. It challenges each of us, regardless of age, to embrace our unlimited potential and take charge of our destinies. It reminds us that the power to transform our lives lies within our grasp, waiting to be ignited by a burning desire for greatness.

So, my friends, are you ready to embark upon this journey, embrace the timeless wisdom shared within these pages and create a world where age is revered and seniors are celebrated as the vibrant, dynamic forces they truly are? I believe in you, in your potential, and in the limitless possibilities that await. Get ready to rewrite the story of aging and unleash the ageless power within all of us.

Darren Stephens
#1 International Bestselling Author of *The Success Principles*

CONTENTS

INTRODUCTION

Are you the kind of person who wants to be in control of your future?

Is your body keeping score, and you feel an inner sense that you want to try something new?

What are you going to do with the extra twenty to thirty years, now that we know we are living longer?

Are you ready to live your life at the right speed and the right tempo, instead of racing through life?

Does looking at aging as a happy adventure excite you?

Our planet knows how to regenerate itself; would you like to take part?

Would it interest you to know why older people are better at starting a business?

How would you feel about rebranding "senior moments" or "showing your age", to Owning Your Age?

How will you feel when you become a recipient of an avalanche of health, wealth and success?

Imagine what you will hear people say when you look and feel ageless?

Can you picture being unforgettable and turn heads of admiration, at any age?

Can you visualise participating in your own millionaire boot-camp?

Do you believe you can be an "Up to Date Super Ager" and Grow Rich not Old?

Do you believe you can become a "Successful Senior"?

You owe it to yourself to become everything you've ever dreamed of being and of having and doing and receive a "Serve of Success".

I believe this book is for YOU!

> 66
>
> *"Education's purpose is to replace an empty mind with an open one"*
>
> - Malcolm S Forbes

CHAPTER 1

Get On Strong and Hold On

CHAPTER 1

Get On Strong and Hold On

> ""
>
> *"Do not grow old, no matter how long you live. Never cease to stand like curious children before the Great Mystery into which we were born"*
>
> - Albert Einstein

Helen and I parked at the tram station. We had driven the car from our homes though it was only a short drive, but too far for us old fossils to walk. Besides, we were out for a day of pleasure and we wanted to pace ourselves. We were heading for Surfers Paradise, famous for being one of the fun places to hang out on the glitter strip of Gold Coast City which, by the way, has the best beaches in the world.

It was a sparkling day; one you just would not want to miss by being indoors. The fifteen-kilometre trip from my house is quite picturesque, so we decided to travel this journey the way we choose to do everything else in our lives these days and "go via the scenic route", so we rode the "G", or in its proper title, the G-Link light rail.

As we are a tad precious, we thought a no stress stroll from the tram would be rather pleasant, besides we knew that the chances of finding a car park in Paradise on a day like that were remote and we were more likely to find a pop-up store selling rocking horse poo. On arriving at our destination which was one of the many majestic skyscrapers that line the spectacular coastline, we floated through the massive doorway into a very spacious foyer that immediately confirmed that we were in a tropical paradise.

We both expressed a slight sigh of regret that we were leaving the great outdoors. With a half -hearted shrug we 'Mothed' into the elevator and escalated to the dizzy heights of the seventy third floor to an apartment in a matter of seconds.

This was for an auspicious occasion, hosted by my friend and fellow author to launch her new book series. We were greeted at the now flung open doors of a fabulous residence by an extremely friendly yet professional looking senior lady who was beautifully dressed and was delightfully loquacious (to save you scratching your head, someone who talks fluently and easily, and a LOT).

One by one we were introduced to the gathered guests and then hugs and congratulations to our host were given. I noticed that most of the guests were clad in typical Gold Coast style (Casual but Classy) and thankfully not a dripping body from the many pools was in sight, nor were there any salty and sand encrusted bodies from the surf here to dampen the party; not on this occasion anyway.

The room was humming with polite chatter with a serving of enjoyable belly laughs every now and again, you know the old nostalgic type that emerges from a memory from years back, the kind of thigh slapping laugh that makes you feel warm and fuzzy even though you are not in the story, but you can relate.

I ambled over to the patio that was closed in with huge glass windows that show-cased a breathtaking easterly view of the vast Pacific Ocean directly in front of me. My eyes were drawn to the varying colours of blues and greens blending wildly with the white caps of the waves that seemed to drift off into infinity till it reached the horizon and then the sky took over to show off its magnificent colours.

—————————— o0o ——————————

When I looked south, the spectacular vista invited me to view the endless white sandy beaches that scrolled off into the distance, hugging the shoreline proudly and smugly displaying the magnificent homes of the rich and famous, along with holiday homes and cabins and, thankfully, some of the still standing dwellings of the early settlers.

It was such a crystal-clear day that something attracted my attention out of the corner of my eye, and for a brief moment I thought I could see New Zealand, so I snapped out of it and promptly looked in the other direction in case my crazy nephews from across the ditch caught me staring at them.

Looking north there are more of the same wonderful picture postcard views, with the added bonus of the start of the many islands scattered past the State capital, Brisbane. From this point onwards all along the Queensland coast is one of the most spectacular wonders of the world: The Great Barrier Reef. Uniquely this is one of the few structures that can been seen from space.

The view straight down out of the window revealed the several resort pools below looking like sequins glistening in the sun, snuggling into coiffured gardens that lead down to an endless strip of white sand. I felt like an eagle looking down into a miniature village because the roads and the cars were so small.

The west lured my eyes to the mountains that cradled the landscape, drawing my attention to the spectacular waterways of all shapes and designs, the ambling Nerang River standing out from the formed canals that look like a lace doily (ask your Nan), meeting up with the mighty Broadwater, a stretch of water lying between the islands and the endless surf. Living up to its name, the Broadwater is a playground for hundreds of watercrafts that look small from here, but a stroll along the many marinas, will reveal some of the most massive and magnificent yachts in the world; on its banks a myriad of restaurants serving cuisine from around the world.

I was joined in conversation by a very distinguished and interesting couple who shared their incredible stories about their tour of duty as Australian Ambassadors in embassies around the Orient. They had retired and become authors and now resided here in Paradise and we reflected on how wonderful the outcome is when people and nature come together. Oh! I might add at this juncture, they were amused that I shared that I knew that there are more canals here than in Venice.

While we were nibbling and nattering our way through a delicious banquet of healthy tropical delights, we were summoned by the traditional tap on a glass with a fork to get our attention as it was time to applaud our distinguished and talented friend.

When the room became respectfully hushed and the accolades began, I panned around taking my curious mind for a stretch, and I noted that the speakers were stimulating and very forward thinking. Our eminent author had captured many years of our local and national history and had lived through a lot of it herself and the nodding crowd walking down memory lane with her were relating to the experience with such interest.

I gave Helen a nod and a nudge as she is my very close friend and a lot of the time we think alike and oddly enough at the same time, and she had also noticed that there was not a person under fifty in the room. In fact, the majority of us were well past the half a hundred mark. We felt so very much at home among a gathering of Futuristic Thinkers who are still very active, productive and progressive. Not only were they interesting they were also very positive, and not one of them moaning about getting old.

o0o

Without conducting a head count we estimated that there were about sixty people gathered, the oldest being the very much alive couple we were chatting with earlier who were in their nineties. I recognised a very familiar voice that I had heard for many years on radio, a gentleman in his eighties and still working. It was great to put a face to that magnificent voice.

Like ourselves, there was a good number of people in their seventies who were authors, speakers, musicians, artists and the like. Deducing from the brief chats we had with other guests, we estimated they were in their fifties and sixties, some in their seventies and eighties. We learned that they were involved in business or teaching and the arts. Now I am no mathematical genius, but I figured that's roughly about 4000 staggering years of wisdom and experience.

After the book signing, we said our goodbyes and made our way like a couple of old moths back down the elevator then boarded the tram and sat in deep thought while we mentally danced around our experience. My eyes were drawn to a sign in the tram that I had briefly glanced at on the ride in; reading it again had a certain ring to it. It had been rolling around in my head like a spare sock in a tumble dryer, then it hit me - (no not the sock) it was a message from the beyond. It read GET ON STRONG AND HOLD ON!

Now that is the best and timely message for us when we are looking down the barrel of our so- called senior journey for that fifty plus ride on the tram of life.

I have shared this story to make a point: sure, we have been to exotic beaches, glitzy places, high rise buildings, luxury apartments, ridden in modern comfortable transport and rubbed shoulders with the best in far off places. It has become second nature as we have taken it all in our stride and for granted. As they say, "no big deal", BUT listen up!

———————————— oOo ————————————

The point is, the next ride in our lives is the most significant because we have bags of wisdom and experience and so much knowledge in our wheelhouse that we don't have to reinvent the wheel. When we step back and look at our time on the planet, we can see that the generations before us had never experienced so much in such a short time in all of history. So get excited, get ready to sizzle on the next part of our lives. Perhaps it is worthwhile to look into the possibility that the more you explore, the happier you will be. Push back your tendency to continually re-tread the same paths and visit the same old places.

Some Psychologists tell us that THE good life is not all about play, pleasure and ease, nor is it about hard work and accomplishment. It also includes something called "psychological richness" which basically means experiencing and weathering new and challenging experiences.

There is also a new line of research showing that newness and a little discomfort fire up the learning centres in your brain.

Give Your Brain A Nudge

New places and experiences are harder to deal with, so we tend to lean on the old standbys. Sometimes it's a bit difficult and less predictable, but science says they are worth the effort because our brains crave new experiences.

Being involved with something new creates a cue for your brain to establish mental triggers that will boost confidence, improve moods and help us navigate our journey with confidence. Being the master of your own destiny creates a vivid reminder of how fantastic life can be.

-o0o-

Get ON Strong, and Hold ON as the best is yet to come.!!!

——————————————— o0o ———————————————

##

"

> *"The key is not to prioritize what's on your schedule but to schedule your priorities"*
>
> - Stephen Covey

www.MaeRoseMethods.com

CHAPTER 2

Exploring Myths About Aging!
So, Mind the Gaps

CHAPTER 2

Exploring Myths About Aging!
So, Mind the Gaps

"

"I have too many flaws to be perfect, but I have too many blessings to be ungrateful"

- Zig Ziglar

This is just a wild guess, but you are probably having a sneaky read of the first couple of chapters of this book because you glanced at the back cover as most of us do because something caught your eye (and it was not a short person with and umbrella), and you thought it was a nice photo, which led you to read my bio, because let's face it, we are all curious about one another.

After you read on a little you silently said to yourself, "She is how old? and she can still fog up a mirror? And she has still got enough marbles to hold a pen the right way up? And can still string a few words together to make a sentence?"

Well, let me tell you, my mind is still like a steel trap, as I distinctly remember having eyebrows and a fully functioning metabolism once, and my baby photos were in black and white, and the nearest telephone was at the post office! I am now thinking that you are more than a bit nosy about how I claim to know a little bit about hitting the reset button on Aging and Money Myths; let's be honest - it was in the back of your mind.

---
oOo

Firstly, let's start with aging. It may be cold comfort to you, but let me assure you that the one thing I have had experience in is aging, so if you are still interested, pull up a chair, grab a cuppa and let's have a chat.

You must be a tad curious about when we start to age; have you ever given it much thought? Or have you given it a lot of thought and it scares you, and you may be in fear that life is passing you by. Are you full of regret about the things you did not do, or the words you did not say, or the feelings you did not express? We certainly don't want to talk about it as there is an embedded stigma attached to getting old because it stirs up a lot of mystique, which is a cleverly disguised word for denial or fear.

Well, I know how you feel as I have felt the same way and I know many others who think and feel that it may be over for them and their dreams and aspirations may be lost because they have run out of time. Now may be a good time, and also may be within your best interests, to have a thought or two on the subject, before you really do leave yourself a short runway.

In my research I asked a lot of people of different ages their thoughts, on what age do they think is considered to be the start of old age, and to my amazement most were none the wiser and could not give a definitive answer, just a stab at a range between fifty to hundred. I noted that they answered fast and scurried away with head down as if the subject was taboo.

On reflection, I thought my Nan was really old when she was in her sixties, and I thought Grandad was as old as Moses because he had a moustache. If anyone was older, they never mentioned it, especially females as it was a cardinal sin to even ask or even infer a lady's age.

Annoyingly, people still think like that to this very day, as to my horror and the detriment to my blood pressure, I recently heard a person on TV talk about their very old mother who was in her seventies. Well excuse me!!!I gave him a Goggle-Box piece of my mind!

———————————————— o0o ————————————————

Delving a little deeper into my interviews I found a common denominator in the majority of the feedback. The age sixty-five came up again and again and when I asked why that age? The reply was unanimous, "because that's when they told us we had to retire". Now I don't know about you but I have heard that for as long as I can remember. In fact, I believed it myself. I heard people declare with gusto that they couldn't wait to retire and live the good life, and we still hear that today.

I feel that you and I are on the same page and we want to know who 'they' are and why did 'they' come up with that emotional jail term? What is scary is how effective it has been to blackmail and brainwash most of the population for so long. The words 'told' and 'retire' in the one sentence tends to rattle my undercarriage somewhat.

This fierce memory of mine clearly recalls how I felt when they told me that. I think you will get a kick out of my story I wrote in another book and it may be a head 'Nodder' for you.

My Rude Awakening Story

On September 17th, 2009, I was rushing about the house like the queen of business as usual, riding three horses in the circus, balancing a ball on my nose and a spoon on top of that, a hoop on each arm spinning plates on sticks and still open to anyone wanting something done. Hypothetically that is, as I have never been on a horse, but the rest fits, and I am sure you can relate to the same juggling act.

A letter I had received in the mail had been sitting on my desk for a couple of days as I was too busy being busy to open it. It had a window on the front and a government crest on the right-hand side. I thought I had better open it as it could be important. A million thoughts stampeded through my mind when I read the official introduction. "Dear Mrs. O'Connell", it began. My still busy mind jumped the gun and wondered had I been doing a hundred and fifty in a sixty zone, again? Had I run over someone's dog? Had I been finally conscripted into the Army?

With now some obvious unstable body parts, I read on as I was still wildly curious about the contents of the letter. It went on to say, "Please find enclosed your Seniors Card." Seniors Card? What Senior's card? I immediately assumed that there was some horrible mistake.

I read on with a very indignant air, with intentions of amending this gross government error and giving them a piece of my mind. Through the steam I read, "Now that you are sixty-five years of age, you are entitled to the Old Age Pension and a concession on the bus".

I was mortified and frozen to the spot as I became increasingly aware that some of my other once totally reliable body parts started to give up on me. Gasping and wheezing I was desperately trying to identify the guttural dragon-like noise emitting from me that sounded like a plate of Mung beans negotiating its way through a cow's lower colon. SIXTY-FIVE! No one told me I was old—when did this happen?

Well, I was on my feet and running around in ever decreasing circles till I took off and started to hover around the house like a military surveillance drone looking for evidence of my senior status. As I became vocal in a deafening way, running for their lives, my left-brained family took cover under the bed.

I was most insulted as I never catch the bus and as an ex-rally driver the mere thought of catching the senior's bus was a massive blow to my normally pristine ego. After the panic and the hysteria died down, my violated ego slumped into a mental deck chair, and I had a very stern talk to my inner snob, took a breath and listened to my heart.

My heart was crying out, "Wait a minute I have not finished yet! I have not fulfilled all of my dreams". I was at the beginning of the "Gaps" that I was not expecting.

Up to this stage my life appeared to be seamless, moving from one experience to another. Childhood, education, career, family, then boom,

—— o0o ——

retirement. It is a huge shock after you have been travelling along on the journey of life at a reasonable pace for 40 to 50 years or so, then you come to a screeching halt.

You find yourself standing on the edge of a cliff gazing at the other side of a gaping hole in your life, holding onto a letter from the government, that letter informs you that you are now entitled to "age benefits". Your sub-conscious mind immediately tracks back in history when it was called the "old age pension", and that was not that long ago.

The words old, pension, and retire, attach to parked emotions, for example, the fear of being obsolete or passed it. It's terrifying because we are not prepared for anything other than conditioning from old paradigms. We have been educated into accepting that, if you have not got your life together by retirement age, it's too late.

It's interesting how all of a sudden wherever you go, you start to notice signs that say "mind the gap", I have adopted it as a metaphor, I now use to be aware of situations that pop up out of the blue that create unexpected gaps in what was once an unbroken chain of events.

> 66
>
> *"It's the stage you are at, not the age you are at"*

With this particular big gap staring me in the face, and one of many I have experienced since, I began to think there was another side to this, I thought maybe I was now free to fly, but then I wondered why does the thrill of soaring begin with the fear of falling? It's ironic how an old paradigm pops out from behind a dream and re-visits your fear.

o0o

Then I remembered that even Eagles need a push. I realised the past cannot be changed, but I can change tomorrow by my actions and attitude today.

I decided to make peace with myself, and reflect upon the positive side of the past and reflect upon what I had learned. I realised that I could look back to understand my life, and now choose to live my life in a forward direction and dare to dream and work to win.

Think about what you can offer the world because of what you know. Charles F. Kettering stated

> "My interest is in the future, because I'm going to spend the rest of my life there"

www.MaeRoseMethods.com

o0o

CHAPTER 3

Living Younger Longer

CHAPTER 3

Living Younger Longer

"
"Even if you don't believe in miracles, perhaps you've forgotten you are one"

- Mae-Rose

Time flies, the years go by like months and, before you know it, you have hit the half century mark. You have not noticed that fifty years go by because you have had a family and or a career, perhaps interests or hobbies filled your life.

Either way, time does not wait, because before you know it, the big "SIX O" pops up uninvited over the hedge and yells, "Surprise!" Then Bingo! "Sixty-Five" head-butts you into the morbid reality that your working life is supposed to be over.

Many of us at this point perhaps fall into the semi-retirement category, but more often than not, at this stage in one's life, people are seeking gratification. You have worked around 40 years or more and are at an unfamiliar intersection that indicates that you are supposed to slow down about now.

But the mere thought of it scares the living daylights out of you and you feel lost. Don't worry about it for too long as the sneaky "Seven O" appears from out of nowhere and grabs you between the handkerchief and the small change. That will take your mind off the fact that that ship has sailed. Then as luck would have it, you'll be waiting at the airport for your "Eight O" ship to come in. Then from there, 'they' put us in the "and Beyond" category, or the "where no one will touch them" department.

Research says we are living longer, and in some parts of the world people are living to one hundred and thirty years of age plus. In one particular village they are all past the age of ninety and are still very productive, self-sufficient and most of all, extremely fit and healthy.

The human race seems to have taken a full circle, as way back in history many people lived into their extreme hundreds. All this time I really thought Methuselah was a fictional character, however the lovely Mrs. Google informed me that he was real and he died aged 969 years. His wife Edna apparently recorded his "stats" because she was a forward-thinking kind of gal, and knew we would be riveted knowing he was born in the morning in 687 BC and popped off the twig in a morning of 1656.

I was curious as to what her age was, as I want whatever it was, she was having. Sadly no "stats" on dear old Edna or her skin care regime.

Just recently our Gold Coast City Mayor stated in a local magazine that the number of seniors is predicted to double by 2031. Compared to other cities around the world, we have a small population, so the mind boggles as to how the system will cope when the world-wide explosion will be at the highest level ever in history. Fortunately for our city, our forward-thinking Mayor has that covered.

As it stands now, we have a considerable number of people who retired at sixty-five, some earlier, some later. Of course, it is considered a well-earned rest for some and they are happy to unwind and relax, take up their favourite hobby or pastime more fully, travel or spend more time with their family. Sadly however, for some others it is a time of loss as they may have loved their career or job and still felt useful and productive.

———————————————— o0o ————————————————

Now they are left grieving and feeling empty because they have been told that their services are no longer required, and then are faced with a tradition or policy that has not changed in decades or if ever.

Their exit certificate was coldly marked D.C.M. (Don't Come Monday) by order of T.F.P. (The Faceless People). So now we are labelled for the rest of our lives as pensioners which immediately puts us in the too hard basket, and in some nasty sectors we are considered a burden and a menace to society. In my case I say, "YES isn't that fabulous?" especially to being a menace.

The MYTH was created long ago, that when we reach that certain age, we had to be herded into the outer paddock out of the way, to stoop and graze and learn the art of being bewildered, which some of us mastered very well and all too quickly. So a huge gap was created from the dreaded sixty-five bingo number till death do us a part.

Let's talk about those in another group that still worked other than in a career or a job, but they worked longer, in fact may be still at it, as they have a business. For some reason, it is not thought of as a job because it is not nine to five, the doors may be closed but the real work is sometimes going on twenty-four seven behind the scenes. The word retirement is not bandied around because in some cases it is out of the question.

Research says that the largest part of the world population is referred to as the 'working class with an employee mindset'. We have become slaves to the system and are oblivious to the fact that we are just lab rats going round and round the wheel. This takes up most of our time for very little, and if we want more, we have to work harder and longer, leaving even less time for anything. It is not our fault: we have been deliberately trained and educated into this thinking by the powers that be for whatever reason. Sadly, we keep that myth alive and accept that this is it, and never challenge the rat race. Keep in mind that even if you win the rat race, you're still a rat.

———————————————————— oOo ————————————————————

So what is society's attitude towards aging? In my research and personal experience, this can vary depending on the cultural, social and economic context in which it occurs. In many societies, aging is often viewed as a negative process and older individuals may be seen as less valuable or less capable than the younger ones. This can result in ageism, or discrimination based on age, which can have negative impacts on the quality of life and well-being of older people.

I could speculate as to why we are living longer. Research says, we are living twenty to thirty-five years longer and there are many theories on the matter. In my interviews most people suggest it may be because of the availability of Allopathic Medicine which is a term to define science-based modern medicine; it has come a long way in the last fifty to a hundred years.

Others say the recognition and application of Ancient Traditional and Complementary medicine which has been around for many years. In Australia we have the privilege of finally respectfully learning and gaining from centuries old bush medicine from our Indigenous First Nations People. Some say it is a combination of all.

There is a very strong opinion that we are much more educated because we are so much more informed. We have access to a wealth of knowledge at our fingertips and almost instantly. No longer do we have to study for years to gain an education, which, in the not-so-distant past, was considered just for the chosen few.

We were educated into having a defeatist attitude. If you did not fit into the hop, skip and jump category (primary school, high school/college, university) you were deemed a Pleb. If you were only average or below at any of the above trio, you were tossed into the loser basket. It even brought shame and embarrassment so we hid in the mundane and flopped along like flotsam and jetsam in the sea of life, or what other term sits comfortably into your particular vernacular.

———————————— oOo ————————————

This abyss created so much unnecessary waste of human intellect and integrity, which in my opinion created a perfect reason to give up early, because there was no other choice. The good news is that there now exists an endless number of opportunities that can put that moth - eaten system out into its own abyss.

Living younger longer. How do we do that in today's fast-moving world and avoid burnout? If your double D cup 'runneth' over, it's time for a spring clean, and we generally get better results if we take everything out and put back only what needs to be there.

> **"**
>
> *"If you want more space, clean out the shed in the back of your mind"*
>
> - Mae-Rose

Many people of all ages, regardless of their status, who had previously thought they had missed out on finding their purpose or fulfilling their dreams and aspirations, are now riding the wave of success. Because of the massive shift in thinking, we are out of the dark ages and into a time of demand, and need for information and education outside of the scholastic system, and we don't have to have titles or be restricted by age to be of value.

Now we are in the driving seat to fill that gap, by creating more space.

Before telling ourselves that creating more space mentally and physically is impossible, it is important to challenge this thought and consider what steps you can take to build more margin into our lives.

In the short-term we seemed like we were working non-stop, staying up late and filling every waking moment with some sort of activity because we thought that was the key to productivity. However, in the long-term, this approach can lead to melt down and burn-out.

All we are left with is exhaustion and a decline in our overall well-being. To avoid burn-out we need to create a space to think. We also need the time to think because time is our most precious commodity, and it is essential to use it and respect it wisely and create a life by design.

The irony is that if we are to be more productive, to come up with good ideas and reach good decisions, we need to slow down and do less. Take advantage of the Double Ds by looking at:

Decelerating - slowing down or stopping, taking time out just to pause and be. Most of all, look ahead into your extended timeline and design what you would like it to look like. Slowing down is to be feared no more.

Decompressing - letting off the pressure. A great way to release pressure in the brain is by writing things down, removing the need to hold everything at the front of the mind. Rearrange your mental deck chairs, let life back in, open the window to new life.

I would add Defiance to the list and make it a triple whammy! Push back at the antiquated attitudes of the past. Come out of the dark ages and work in the light, away and above that ancestral programming. Don't lie about your age, instead boast about it—and smile when their jaws drop in amazement when they learn that you can jump out of bed in the morning and see yourself a decade younger in the mirror.

YOU ARE HERE: Taking away the programming is wonderful and uplifting, it's a start, but not a complete solution, nor is it a quick fix. Imagine that you have a very grand house, it looks amazing and beautiful at a glance, and you have just learnt the foundations were not built to hold up such a magnificent structure.

—————————————————— o0o ——————————————————

To pull the foundations out would be a disaster, as the house would fall in. Architects, engineers, and planners would have to be contracted to strategically replace load-bearing sections of the foundations, bit by painstaking bit to preserve the building.

So start from here, by acting the age you chose to be right now, keeping in mind that seventy is the new forty. Don't say "I wish" or "I will", as that is acting in the future. Just say with conviction I am aging backwards as I move forward.

Do you remember all of the New Years' resolutions you made and how many you actually kept? Every January you made a long list of intentions, but by February you had delayed the process because you were too busy. By March, you realise they are not going to happen. You become overwhelmed with remorse and self-recrimination. You punish yourself because you have failed, once again, to fulfil the promises you made to yourself, which has an effect on everything around you.

To take the pressure off yourself, think about this. At the time they were made they were only options, as it was not in the now. All good intentions aside, it was still a dream. It was not specific, nor realistic, and that is like pushing and shoving at a locked door.

To make this shift happen and stay locked in as absolute, you need to become your own architect, engineer, builder and planner. Think NOW and grow young. Don't worry about getting old, worry about thinking old.

Liken this scenario to the strengthening of your foundations. It enables you to structure the rest of your light and life on these foundations, for the rest of your life. It gives you an unencumbered future, and the freedom to revisit your hopes, dreams and aspirations, and turn them into reality.

o0o

> ❝
>
> *"You are not too old; you've just mastered the fine art of convincing yourself you are. You are younger than your Tomorrows. Wiser than your yesterdays. Stronger than your excuses. And deserving of a chance"*
>
> - Broms The Poet

www.MaeRoseMethods.com

CHAPTER 4

Age Freezing

CHAPTER 4

Age Freezing

> ❝
>
> *"Separating Fact from Fiction About the Aging Process"*
>
> *"It's never too late for a new beginning"*
>
> - Joyce Meyers

I have found that over the many years in my practice as a Natural Therapist and a Lifestyle Coach, a large proportion of clients who came to my clinic were seeking treatment for various health conditions like depression, tiredness, unexplained aches and pains, digestive problems…the list went on. On many occasions there was no or any real evidence that there something organically wrong.

During that time, I was a dedicated heart 'sleever' and a hopeless 'rescuer' and I wanted to fix everyone, and I was devastated when I could not. I had to find another way, so my intuition and my fierce drive kicked in and hooked up with my training, as a woman and a mother and added a handful of the many other modalities I had studied, to find the root cause and stop treating the symptoms. It was not always easy as the deep-rooted trained patterns were indelibly imprinted into their psyche. The push back was incredibly hard to deal with as I was dealing with minds that are fixated in tradition.

Have you seen or heard of the elephant in the circus held captive by a little rope and a small stake in the ground? We have all seen elephants in the wild moving enormous obstacles out of their path with their incredible strength.

---

oOo

It's because when the elephant was a baby with very little strength, the greedy circus owners tied a rope around an ankle and fastened it to a stake in the ground to stop the animal from roaming. Because it has such a good memory it never forgets the training in captivity which prevents it moving away. Even though it could easily break free it still remains a prisoner of the past.

Even before we age, we are told to expect to become forgetful, depressed, and become more dependent on others because we become less physically active. We are brain-washed into believing that we become less creative. Is it any wonder that we end up giving up, as it seems hopeless, and may as well "play the game"?

There are many myths about aging that are harmful and misleading. That is why I am on a mission to educate, influence, encourage and instil a sense of purpose and value into as many fossils as I can, while I can, to dispel the negative myths that have whiskers on them (if you'll pardon the pun).

Take a few long moments to analyse what is your rope and stake that is keeping you prisoner of your past.

If you have a hint of fire in the belly, and you can still fog up a mirror, and you don't want to be in a jar on the mantelpiece next to Nan and Pop, and it is not your desire to end up pissing yourself in a nursing home, cut the rope and pull out the stake, come with me and we will rattle some cages and shake some trees and rip up the out-dated rules together.

In some societies, older people are respected and valued for their experience and wisdom, and are seen as an integral part of the community. In these societies, there may be a greater emphasis on intergenerational relationships and the role of older people in passing down knowledge and traditions to younger generations.

o0o

In recent years, there has been a growing recognition of the importance of promoting positive attitudes towards aging and the valuable contributions that older people can make to society.

There are also efforts underway to combat ageism and to create more inclusive and age-friendly environments that support the well-being and independence of these awesome human beings - us.

Hang on. Before you race out and jump into a Lycra skin suit and enter the Tour de France, or join the Navy Seals, or become a Pole Dancer, there are a few realistic things you may want to consider.

The aging process is very real and it is the gradual decline in the functioning and ability of an organism to adapt to its environment as it gets older. It is a complex process that is influenced by a combination of genetic, environmental and lifestyle factors.

The aging process can be divided into two main categories: cellular and physiological.

Cellular Aging refers to the gradual decline in the function and integrity of cells over time. This can lead to a range of age-related changes at the cellular level, such as the loss of DNA repair mechanisms, the accumulation of cellular damage and the decline in the production of essential molecules.

Physiological Aging refers to the changes that occur in the functioning of the body's systems as we get older. These changes can affect various aspects of our health, including our physical and mental function, our immune system and our ability to regenerate tissue.

The aging process is a natural part of life, and it is not something that can be stopped as yet. However, there are things that we can do to help the impact of aging on our health and well-being, so that we can really LIVE till we die.

---

oOo

Attitude is the main and essential step to take to grow your wings and fly first class on Wisdom Airlines. My motto is *"If life is a journey and death is inevitable, then I'm going via the Scenic Route."*

"

If life is a journey and death is inevitable,
then I'm going via the Scenic Route"

- Mae-Rose

You are welcome to use my philosophical motto as long as you also apply my G.O.Y.A. principles of action as in "Get Off Your Assets" and seek buoyant mental and physical health and help yourself become interdependent.

By following these tips, you can help to dispel myths about aging and make informed decisions about your health and well- being as you age.

1. Seek out reliable sources of information: Don't rely on hearsay or misinformation. Instead seek out reliable sources of information such as websites of reputable organisations or books written by experts on aging.

2. Don't believe everything you hear: Just because something is widely believed doesn't make it true. Be willing to question what you hear and do your own research to determine the truth.

3. Talk to experts: If you are unsure about something, don't be afraid to reach out to a healthcare professional or other expert on aging for guidance.

---

o0o

4. Be open to new ideas: It can be hard to let go of long-held beliefs, but it is important to be open to new ideas and to consider different perspectives.

5. Also be open to old ideas: Don't rule out that a lot of the time Granny was right and her methods worked and still do when sometimes all else fails.

6. Practice critical thinking: When you hear a myth about aging, take a moment to consider whether it makes any sense or if it might be too good to be true. Be willing to question what you hear and think critically about it.

7. To create space for inspiration, remove destructive dialogue from your programming, for instance "I am over the hill", "Past your prime", "Finished at forty", "One foot in the grave", "Showing my age".

8. Resist this ageist attitude as it reeks of decline.

9. Move out of reaction and move into the power of reflection.

10. Regard aging as a Super Power.

Let me introduce you to a couple of Attitude Queens, two fabulous ladies who were poles apart in every way. Both were mentors in my life, neither of them are celebrities nor were they famous, but they both made a tremendous impact in my life in their own special way.

Rita Amelia, my beautiful mother-in-law, was aged 98.75 when she passed, Jessie Rose, my mother, was aged 94.95 when she passed. They were like tuning into a couple of old radio stations, smooth and easy listening.

Rita Amelia, my valued and beloved mother-in-law, was a beautifully soft and well-spoken elegant, attractive lady who emigrated from England as a child and lived in New Zealand. She was always impeccably dressed in perfectly tailored clothes, a tad conservative, but colour co-ordinated to suit every occasion. Her soft grey hair was coiffured always and never a hair out of place. On a damp day she wore one of those concertina rain hats that tie under the chin, taking every caution not to spoil the hair doo. Every day without fail, on rising she dressed and put her make-up on and donned her very well-chosen jewellery, even if she was working in her rose garden. She had a very Windsor-like politeness about her, and never seemed to lose her cool. Her last words of wisdom to me taught me about perspectives. I asked her if she was looking forward to receiving her letter from the Queen on the 100th Anniversary of her birth. In her very dulcet tone, she replied "My dear Mae-Rose, when that day arrives it won't be the same as there will be a King. Almost to that very day the Queen passed. It is a day I will never forget with such fond memories of Rita Amelia.

Jessie Rose, now that is another story, she was like a number nine cyclone, she would be up before everyone else, daks rolled up, walking around in bare feet sweeping the path, looking like a smile on a stick. "Hatchet Face", as we used to fondly call her, was born in Mackay, Queensland. Her mother emigrated from England as a child. Her father was Australian born to Chinese parents.

Her gift was bringing people together as she loved to organize and get things moving. There was never a dull moment as she was a mover and a shaker. She was a bit of a "Bossy Boots", in fact would have made a good prison warden. I dragged her around the world with me in my travels buying fabrics and we had such a lot of fun.

Before she retired at 82, she would go off to her little dressmaking and gift shop business for a full working day, then in the evening, dress up

---

oOo

---

to the nines and hit the dance floor where she taught Ballroom Dancing for many years. In her ball gowns she looked stunning as she was a beautiful looking woman with an effervescent personality, loved a laugh and loved everyone. Her pearls of wisdom were, when somebody asked why she never remarried, "Why make one man miserable when I can make so many happy?". My add on was, "she can whizz them around the dance floor, pat them on the head and send them home, and that way she does not have to iron the peg marks out of his underpants." Like Mother, like Daughter. It's all about attitude.

Working as a Clinician in my early years opened my eyes and my heart about having a positive attitude towards aging. Some would come in for acupuncture, or a massage, a lot of the time they would come in for colon hydrotherapy, or some emotional clearing or an eye rolling foot reflexology session.

One particular old Darling Doris in her late nineties made me laugh when preparing her chart. I asked several questions then asked her if she and her husband had children, she said no not yet we are still trying. Never as long as I live will ever forget her phrase, "Many a good tune is played on an old fiddle".

There was no secret to these incredible beings living younger longer: their attitude was always there for all the world to see. Most of all it was the life stories they shared.

oOo

"

"I love getting older. My understanding deepens, I can see what connects, I can weave stories of experience and apply them. I can integrate the lessons. Things simply become more and more fascinating. Beauty reveals itself in a thousand forms"

- Victoria Erickson

www.MaeRoseMethods.com

CHAPTER 5

Money Myths

CHAPTER 5

Money Myths

> **"**
>
> *"The truth about what it takes to become wealthy"*

Have you secretly asked yourself, why are you not as wildly successful financially as others you look up to?

Do you look in the mirror and wonder why you are not highly paid and in demand in your field?

Have you ever said, "Oh if I could only win the Lottery, then all my problems would be solved"?

Do you blame lack of money for your problems?

I know how you feel as I have felt the same way, and I have discovered so many people who have struggled with these very limiting beliefs.

Where did these beliefs come from and when did they start to have a negative impact on so many?

When I was researching this very complex topic, I heard the same old stories and phrases from people as if they were raised by a parrot. I know because a little birdie told me the same things over and over until I was able to know them off by heart. In fact, give me a cracker and play a jingle and I will recite them without a hitch and throw in a little dance.

You know the old chestnuts: "Do you think I am made of money"? It was more like a questionnaire and not a statement. As a child I was worried sick about solving the mystery about what my father was made out of, it was complete confusion to me as I didn't even know what money was made from, let alone how he was put together. I thought I had to come up with the answer.

"Do you think money grows on trees"? Was another probing question. I was a nervous wreck as I was forever checking under the mango tree in our backyard for loose change, and looking up into the branches for dollar bills. In my pea brain I thought it was just another skill I was being trained in, to one day become a professional hoop jumper. My self-doubt was being nurtured at the same time, as he scolded me and told me I was stupid for planting feathers to grow chickens.

My father was a highly educated man, in fact he was a mathematical genius. He started to study Agriculture at University; World War II broke out before he could graduate and he joined the Army. Because of his skills he moved up the ranks and became an officer. He never told us much about his military status other than he started as a Drill Sergeant and a few other titles which I can't remember, but the one I do recall, he was an ace marksman. He also served in the Royal Australian Air Force. After the war he worked in the mining sector for several years, then with the surveyors' department in the Gold Coast City Council.

Without using a calculator as they were not readily used on the job by workmen back then, and just using a note-book, he could work out complex figures in his head, he could measure how much coal was in an underground seam within an ounce, and the location within an inch. When later working with the surveyors, they were baffled as to how he could measure land mass without the aid of a Theodolite.

oOo

My point of mentioning these facts is that how can a person with such a razor-sharp mind be brain-washed enough to have the power to unknowingly instil these damaging myths about money into the underdeveloped mind of a child?

Now I realise how powerful the system was back then to bypass the value of loyal hard-working people and bring them to their knees and inject them with a scarcity consciousness. What is more terrifying is that it is a belief system still standing to this very day.

Living through the pain of the generations before me I now utilize my adult reasoning and understand it was not their fault. Tracing back further into my family history, I remember his father, my grandfather, was a soldier in the 1st Light Horse Brigade in World War I and the Diggers, on their return, were left to survive the best way they could. My grand-parents on both sides, along with the majority of Aussies at the time, suffered through the Great Depression. Before they could recover, World War II was upon them.

Stepping back and looking at it now, we did not stand a chance against those odds. The positive news is that from this day forward we can take control as it is time to bury those out-dated myths. We are in a time of revelation, change and growth, there is an abundance of opportunities that don't require degrees or titles. What is positive and exciting, there is no age limit, so anyone who choses can succeed.

The great news is our world has become so much more transparent and accessible and the information highway links us to untold opportunities. The advent of Artificial Intelligence and electronic learning are no longer considered science fiction.

So... what is Money?

––––––––––––––––––––––––– oOo –––––––––––––––––––––––––

Money is the method we use as a means of exchange to give and receive, to earn or trade, or to invest. It is a value system, a tool or utensil that is an incredible servant. Money is an exchange mechanism in society. Money does not make you into anything in particular, but what it does do is simply magnify what you already are.

Let's consider some of the options of how to procure money, or more to the point how we have been trained to think are the only ways.

- You can win it
- You can find it
- You can steal it
- You can wish for it
- You can inherit it
- You can invest it
- You can earn it

Winning the Lottery is every person's fantasy. Your chance in a pool of over 250 million is 0.00001%. The statistics say that is about the same percentage of people who will actually hang onto the money even if they do win. In reality it is a fantasy with little substance.

"Money doesn't grow on trees", was the family mantra. There was a time in history when some money was made out of paper from the trees, that is maybe where that little chestnut came from. So the chances of finding millions of dollars are very low with less than lottery odds.

Stealing money is not a recommended alternative. The original gain is short lived, if and when you get caught. I could be wrong; you may enjoy that kind of vacation in a room without a view and a set menu. Who am I to judge as you may have a two for one deal and been there before.

———————————————— o0o ————————————————

Some believe you can meditate, visualise, tap, sit and pray to attract money. I hear that this has actually happened to a chosen few. At the end of the day, you still have to acquire the skills of discipline and focus, plus have the time to do so. Alas, the average 'Doris' thinker like me would have more chances of becoming an Astronaut. Mind you, it is not out of the question.

Inheriting it is just like a family lottery, the odds are stacked up against you as the majority of people have very little left over from a lifetime of just getting by. There are in some cases a reasonable inheritance left to a family or a benefit that is utilised properly. Mostly however the amount is not enough for a Villa by the sea, but more usually it is absorbed into an easier system of getting by a little better.

Investing is an excellent option to earn more money, but the snag is, you have to have some first. Options like real estate, commodities, businesses etc. require specialized knowledge and skills in these fields. If you had that kind of knowledge already, you probably would not be reading this book.

The good news is earning money and investing it, bar none, may be the most practical and fastest, perhaps the easiest way to build wealth.

What money is NOT.

Some people think that money is like a pond, but like water if it does not move it will stagnate. There is no inlet or any outlet, meaning that some people hold on to it and don't spread it around and save it for a rainy day.

Ask yourself, do you use it or does it use you? A very famous person once said, "Money is like manure, if you hoard it, it eventually stinks. If you spread it around it will make things grow".

o0o

No doubt you have heard the old long running scare tactic "Money is the root of all evil". As we well know today, that phrase was misquoted to control the people of the world. It actually reads "The LOVE of money is the root of all evil". How interesting and powerful that one word carefully misplaced, can hold us hostage for most of our lives.

It's your attitude towards money that determines the effect of money in your life, it's not money itself. How many people do you know who do not have a brass razoo or two pennies to rub together, yet they love money.

On the other hand, there are people who do have lots of money and you never hear them say they love money.

For money to grow it has to circulate, it has to move, therefore let it flow in and flow out like the tide. Be more than generous, invest in education of yourself and others. Prosperity will flow like a river as there is an abundance of all things, and plenty to go around, when you fall in love with the process.

What if I told you there is nothing mysterious about earning a high income, and what if it was as simple as just following systems. The easy part is that it is a present, meaning "Pre-Sent" opportunities that have already been designed and proven to work. All you have to do is hook them up to desire and commitment.

We are experiencing, right now, the most significant wealth transfer in all of human history and you are free to capitalize on it to dramatically improve your ability to prosper in every area of your life.

When I decided to branch out and add to my existing career, and to upgrade my financial status, I asked the kind Mrs. Google what career and financial opportunities are available for seniors. Thinking there would be only a few if any, I was not all that hopeful.

—————————————————— o0o ——————————————————

To my surprise and almost disbelief I found literally hundreds of simple join the dots programs all ready for you. All you have to do is ease your essence into it, put your mark on it, and place it in front of the market. Not only is it fun, it's exciting, and I am sharing it with you and I have named this baby, my **EPP:** easy wealth creation for seniors in three easy steps - **Ease, Put, Place**.

Many of you have toiled and worked hard for most of your life, so you already know that hard work is not the answer to anyone's money problems.

If you are truly committed and not just interested (two different realities) and you are prepared to follow shortcuts used by millionaires and top entrepreneurs, this could be music to your ears.

Reprogram your brain for wealth with a new Brain Hack. Re-work, re-imagine, rewire, re-boot. This will erase seemingly impossible changes to give you a gut reaction of prosperity by erasing negative responses.

Fixing your money hard drive in a therapeutic way, naturally converts into higher levels of success into the landscape of your subconscious mind.

> **"**
>
> *"Money can't buy happiness, but poverty can't buy anything"*
>
> - Dr. E. Richard Friedman

www.MaeRoseMethods.com

CHAPTER 6

The Seniors Wealth Map

CHAPTER 6

The Seniors Wealth Map

> **"**
>
> *"Creative Ways for Seniors to Maintain Financial Freedom"*

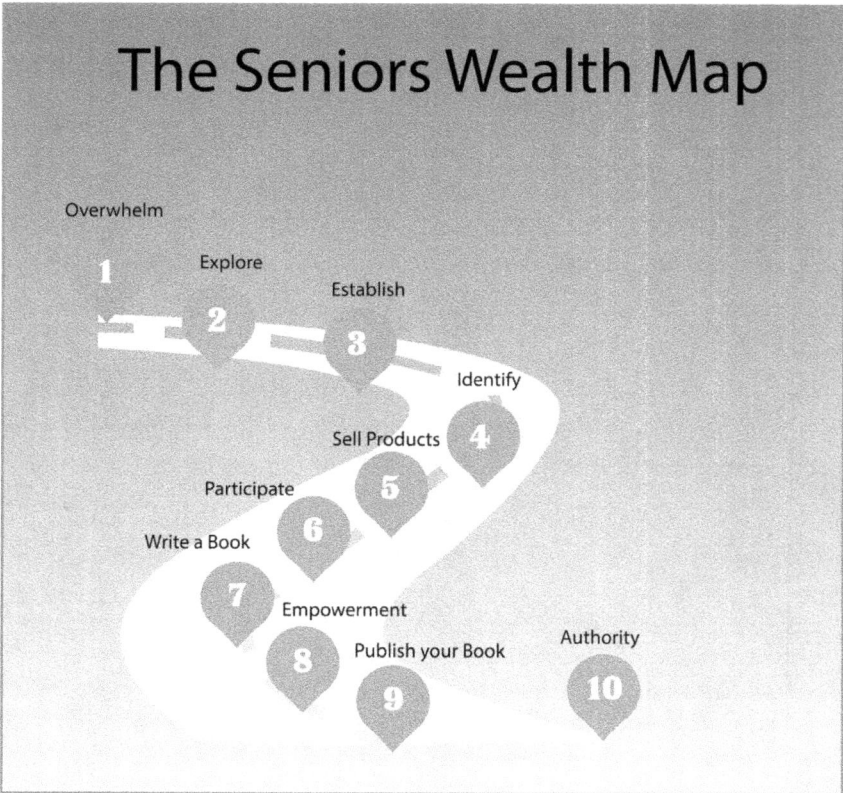

The Seniors Wealth Map

Overwhelm
1
Explore
2
Establish
3
Identify
4
Sell Products
5
Participate
6
Write a Book
7
Empowerment
8
Publish your Book
9
Authority
10

> 66
>
> *"Wealth is not a matter of intelligence, it's a matter of passion and persistence"*
>
> - Darren Stephens

What happens to our psyche when we mention the "M" word? The mind immediately goes into panic mode, and in times of crisis we speak in fluent cliché. Money does not grow on trees. Money does not stick to me, money, have I none, money, money, money. There is a glaring connection between our finances and our feelings.

What would happen if we changed the clichés? "IF you think you are financially stuck, think again, you are using old solutions". "You are not a **has-been**; you are an **about-to-be**". "If you can't see your vision yet, borrow mine".

Step One. OVERWHELM. Many seniors want to work, and the statistics say there is at least half a million vacancies available at any given time. So what is the problem? One problem is most governments let you work for one day then tax you the rest, and if you are entitled to a pension, you will lose it, plus you sacrifice the benefits (like a free ride on the bus). So what is the solution?

Step Two. Let's EXPLORE the possibilities. Have you thought that maybe you are trying to find solutions to the wrong problems? One possibility is you could update your mindset and seek out the right solutions for the presenting problems. You could connect with your dollar thinking software and utilise the portable asset right above your nose (your brain). Decide to spend time with opportunities to uncover your blind spots by educating yourself to be open to opportunities.

Step Three. Let's ESTABLISH that it is possible to profit from your skills, dreams and passions. Surprise yourself and write a list of the things you can do, the things you love to do, and the things you would like to do. Simply, all you have to do is share that knowledge with those who want it.

Turn your passion into a career and teach others. Younger people today have no idea what you know, also there are people reaching a senior age who may know, but don't know what to do with their experiences. Adding your valuable content could make a world of difference to so many in need.

Step Four. Identify your skills and talents and area of expertise. This could be a hobby, past or present profession, or something you are passionate about. If you don't want to start a business you could become a tutor or a mentor and offer your services to existing companies or businesses.

Step Five. Selling products and services related to your passions is a great way for seniors to share their knowledge and skills and potentially turn it into a business. For example, you may be into gardening, cooking, fitness, sport, finance, real estate, medical, teaching, the list is endless. You could turn these priceless assets into a consulting service or create an online course.

Step Six. You can create or participate in online forums, social media groups, or virtual meet-ups to connect with others and share their knowledge and skills. You can sell affiliate products and programs online and never physically handle a single item.

Step Seven. I have saved the best till last, WRITE A BOOK! You already have the content on several interesting and motivational topics. I would wager that you could talk for hours on something you love. I would even go as far as to guess that, at least one time, you have said I could write a book about it. Look at the statistics, there are several hundred million seniors longing to extend their lives and knowledge.

Why don't they get it from YOU!

Imagine how you would feel if you could touch the hearts and minds of just a portion of that huge number. From your book, you can interest them in your online courses or products and services. Ask yourself is there anyone on this planet that has your exact personality, charm, talents and experience?

Step Eight. Now that we have removed the "Dis-tractor" implants, it is safe to use the word EMPOWERMENT. By asking the right questions (How do I do it? When can I start?) will get you excited and results driven and ready to sizzle. Your exuberance will attract the perfect opportunities as you will stand up and stand out.

Step Nine. There are two paths you can take to achieve your goals.

Path one: Do-It-Yourself (DIY) path. It is possible to do it on your own because you are capable and you have the time. But you have been on this solo journey for some time, long enough to realise that your time is your biggest priority.

Path two: Done-For-You (DFY), or Done-With-You (DWY) offers.

Done-For-You solutions are a great option for individuals or businesses that want to maximise efficiency and convenience. With our DFY solution, your task can be escalated by hiring one of our Virtual Assistants, you simply hand over a task to a professional, and they take care of everything for you. This means that you can focus on your core business while still benefiting from the expertise of professionals.

The benefits of hiring a virtual assistant (VA) is they are typically highly skilled and experienced individuals who can handle a variety of tasks, from administrative work to technical support. This means that you can free up your time to focus on your next project. Reference: MaeDazeMillion$Marketing.com

Done-With-You is an even greater solution: It includes all of the above with the added bonus of having our professional team work closely with you to help you choose the right project to fit your personality and topic. We would put you in the direction of a publisher to write your million-dollar best seller book. This team of established experts, will guide you every step of the way to becoming a Best-Selling Author, which is guaranteed to fast track your credibility.

Reference: GlobalPublishingGroup.com.au

Step Ten. Plan where and when you want to be positioned. Choose where you would like to start. Maybe one or more of the above suggestions appeals to you or you may have something already planned.

Visualise what it would look like, perhaps you can see yourself autographing your best seller book, or promoting your book at a seminar. Your dream may be to have a very successful internet marketing business, designing other people's businesses. Affiliate marketing may interest you, where you market other people's products and services and earn a good living from commissions.

When you have identified the direction you want to go, and you have found an interesting way to create your wealth pathway, it is important to place yourself in front of the market-place. Building a relationship with your potential audience takes time: you have to earn their trust and respect. Instead of taking years to build a rapport with your customers in a crowded market place, you can fast track by creating your own personal brand.

-o0o-

————————————————— o0o —————————————————

As we all know, repetitive advertising is very hypnotic. Just think about it when you may want a coffee, or a burger or a meal of any kind; a quick mental checklist can immediately come up with a picture of a logo or a slogan. We don't always think of cars, boats, homes, boy's toys, handbags, shoes, fashion, bling - we think IN Brands and Logos.

Positioning yourself along with your product or services will create a distinct identity and valuable proposition that sets you apart from competitors in the minds of your target audience. It will distinguish you from the others even in the same field by clarifying your unique value that you offer.

Speaking of offers, if you are open to a new and exciting opportunity and are interested in seeing why others are leaving their jobs or careers, take the Free Tour and add your best email address in the following link. It costs nothing to look around: https://livegoodtour.com/maerose

❝

"If someone offers you an amazing opportunity and you're not sure you can do it, say yes – then learn how to do it later"

- Richard Branson

-o0o-

BRANDING refers to the process of creating a stand-alone identity or image. One that propels you forward, and over and above the madding crowd. It involves developing a name, logo, design, a message with an overall strategy that differentiates you and or your products and services. It communicates value to your avatar.

oOo

The goal of branding is to create a strong and positive perception of you and your offers which will lead to brand awareness, customer loyalty, and ultimately, greater business success.

The customer always thinks "What's in it for me" (WIIFM), so you need to pay attention to their needs, values and behaviours. Do some research and create your customers' personas, these should include demographic information, as well information such as their values, interests, and behaviours.

The potential clients' WIIFM is testing to see if that can be achieved through you. They need to feel confident immediately that you are to be trusted and competent to deliver to them their needs. You then have to be very solid in standing in your own persona by knowing yourself.

KNOW YOURSELF. I am sure you have heard that before. You may be wondering what has that got to do with the price of eggs. Believe it or not it has everything to do with it. Have you ever wondered that when we meet or greet a person, the first thing we do is look them straight in the eye, and mostly they look at ours.

If that does not happen it's over, forget it, there will be no exchange of words that will gain trust.

So even a well-rehearsed script, or your million-dollar message will be unheard if you have not got their interest oozing from your eyes and your body language. You have also no doubt heard that the eyes are the window to the soul. They give out instant information like a cosmic fax or a post.

The majority of people you come in contact with can read you, even if they don't know it. They may feel or sense something about you that influences their reaction with you. WOW! What power you have.

— oOo —

Your eyes, your body language and your dialogue have the power to depict who you are and what your persona is, so in a nutshell you won't have to sell a thing, people will want to have what you're having and how you are doing it. Your X factor will magnetically interest them enough to want the product or service you are offering.

They will be intrigued by your Verb. Discovering your Verb is a simple task that deletes the clutter and ensures your message and brand stands alone, as it makes it very clear. This also cuts out the needless noise as your Verb says it all.

Haruki Murakami once said once, "I move, therefore I am"; I love the quote by August Strindberg "I dream therefore I exist". One of the greatest scientific minds of the twentieth century Albert Einstein uttered the following words that still holds true to reality today. "Nothing happens until something moves".

I love to inspire, so my Verb becomes "I inspire, therefore I am". I found out why it was my Verb, as it is my desire and passion to reach out to you as a mentor and inspire YOU to discover who you really are and discover your Verb. It will help you to get to know yourself and live in your Verb to engage better with others.

Ask around, get your friends, family, neighbours or work colleagues to describe you in one word, a verb. What is it you do when you are at your best, what is your action, your state of being? Do you drive, exist, think, listen, invent, plan, play, imitate, love, muse?

"

Albert Einstein said *"Nothing happens until something moves"*

o0o

So move everything out and only put back what is beneficial, so you can progress unencumbered towards your goals. Unclutter your pathway so you can move forward and succeed.

They say that first impressions count, and a picture paints a thousand words. Who do you look for in a group photograph? If you are honest, you always look for yourself first. Why? One reason could be to see how you look, for your own sake. Call it ego if you like in some cases; it may well be. Another point of view is that maybe you care how other people see you.

Both of those points matter when you look at the big picture. Your appearance is important especially now that you are ready to step into the spotlight. You have worked on your mental image, by setting in place where you want to be financially, and how successful you want to be in your chosen new ventures.

To complete the whole picture: it is important to look good. Having a good photographer who is experienced in creating pictures for successful branding and who can also capture the images that suit your project is a valuable investment.

It is not about glamour or centrefold photography. Natural with a few tweaks is a great combination, by using a few props can create a story. If you are an author, you could be holding a copy of your book. Perhaps you are a marketer, pointing towards the future sets a tone. If you are a business person, you would be best placed sitting at a desk or a boardroom table. If you are a freelancer, a backdrop with a beach and palm trees depicts a casual lifestyle. It may be fashion or hairdressing. You could be a sports person, or work with children or animals, nursing if you are a carer.

Become success ready, act as if it is happening now. Having a photographic portfolio at your fingertips is a smart way to start as an

— oOo —

opportunity may come up to start the ball rolling in getting known. Most events and opportunities are booked ahead of time, so even if you do not have your presentation or products ready, you still have a window of time to finish preparations.

Your photographs in some cases are the first introduction to prospective agents so they need to be very professional and depicting at a glance what you represent. Your experienced photographer would have gone through this step by step to achieve the perfect outcome.

Use the right image that tells your story in a glance, and place it on business cards, letterheads, book covers, banners, websites, social media pages. You may have, at some time, merchandise, like pens, notepads, mugs, t-shirts that enhance your brand.

Your bio is part of the whole package, so it needs to be strategically written and to the point. This is where your Verb comes in handy: it cuts out the clutter in your message, as people's attention span is very short in today's market, so make it easy to understand and hit the mark straight off.

Choosing your signature colours is part of the first impressions effect. It also sets the tone of you and your business. Less is more, meaning too many combinations can detract from your message. Colours also stick in the minds of people, and you want them to remember your colours at least, when all else fails.

Attire is part of the package, meaning if you are selling business, choose garments that look business like or in a corporate style. Maybe you are into health, so your branding would have attire and colours that plant the seeds of health in the minds of your potential customers. Fitness, gardening, music, teaching, and so on all have their particular moods.

———————————— o0o ————————————

Let your branding team take worry or stress away from your success. Call us for a complimentary chat about where you want to go and what you want to achieve.

We are the "Million $ Branding Icons"; our years of experience working with celebrities can tell at a glance what is your personal brand, one that is uniquely yours. Spotlighting you to be a sought-after, Go-To Person in your field.

YOU are the answer and there will never be another YOU. Become a "Successful Senior" by partnering with our successful team to bring out the hidden Legend in you.

> ❝
>
> *"If you want one year of prosperity, grow seeds. If you want ten years of prosperity, grow trees. If you want a lifetime of wealth, grow your self-worth"*
>
> - Chinese proverb.

www.MaeRoseMethods.com

CHAPTER 7

Travel In Style While Having Fun

CHAPTER 7

Travel In Style While Having Fun

"

"The Ultimate Guide for Seniors to Enjoy the Best of Travelling"

Have you ever looked forward to a holiday adventure? Maybe it is the trip of a lifetime, or perhaps you have been excited about attending a long-distance seminar or convention? Do you remember the planning and the preparation? You've been plotting and bragging about it for months or in some cases years with such anticipation and you can't wait to get started.

Everything must be just right, you have checked the tickets, visas and passports (if going overseas), gone over the itinerary a hundred times, packed and repacked the appropriate clothes and a few more just in case.

The bon–voyage party was such fun, everyone is happy for you, even if they are a tad envious, but delighted just the same. You may on the other hand, have had an early night to be fresh for an early start with a run through to make sure you have everything right and double checked.

A trip of any kind can be a fun time for some people and it goes without a hitch, or in some cases can be a dread for others, because it's the getting to the destination that fills them with gloom. I have compared my past experiences with other fellow travellers and a lot of funny and tragic

---

oOo

stories have emerged. Also, after years as a Naturopath I noted that a pattern was evident from clients who had travelled a little and some who had travelled extensively.

In my research I discovered that, like me, others dreaded the journey because it's during the journey some most unpleasant and inhumane things can occur to our vintage bodies. Things that make you think this was a bad idea and all you want to do is to go home.

This little rant applies mostly to flying, but don't rule out driving, caravanning or bussing it, or even in a Sedan chair, if that's how you roll, as for some people it is very real and far removed from the comfort and routine of home.

I have put together a top 10 list of the most common challenges that are hard enough to manage at home let alone in a confined space for hours on end. Headache, swollen legs, insomnia, cramps, aching feet, neck pain, indigestion, bloating, gas, and the big one - constipation.

Just one or two of these nasty holiday fun spoilers can ruin several beautiful moments and make you feel you have been banished to the skies to be punished.

Over a few laughs my team and I have compiled a brochure to interest you in flying Wisdom Airlines in the future, where you will be issued with a Triple S visa, with a guaranteed triple F rating. SSS offers Smart, Smooth, Successful Travel. FFF rating ensures you of a Fatigue, and Flatulence Free Flight. Stay with me!! This is for your benefit and with your end in mind.

Before we get to the brochure, let's chat about some of the events that may be part of the problem, and may be preventable in the future. If you have travelled then some of these will be relatable, because the lead up can be exciting or stressful particularly for long distance flights.

o0o

Have you ever left home and on the way to the airport, you have a little panic attack because you have a feeling in the pit of your gut that you have forgotten something, and it goes around and around in your head like it is on a loop? Even though you know you have thoroughly packed the kitchen sink, a step ladder, tent poles, a sturdy rope and a bulging toiletry bag, and yet there is still that fear that you will not enjoy yourself without that extra pair of knickers.

By the time you have dragged your luggage that looks and feels like a herd of swaying mammoths, to the check in desk, your mind rapidly changes from what you thought you may have forgotten to sheer terror - am I overweight? Well, if the truth be known, you probably are, but this time we are talking about the bags. As luck would have it, this time you got the bags through.

With a little party mode reappearing over the chaos, you join the shin kicking contest through security. Now that is fun as you get to partially undress, jacket off, belt off, sometimes shoes off, empty your pockets, phone, watches, small change into a knuckle breaking tray while you drag the lap-top out of the bag and heave it into another lethal weapon. Hands up, turn to the right, turn to the left and you shake it all about, as you shuffle through the X-ray thing.

I always look forward to the next step, it's the push and shove game, as you are waiting for your prized possessions to appear unscathed through the sausage machine. With passport and boarding pass between your teeth, laptop under your chins, that is when you are glad of those few extra chins for a better grip. At this juncture you are grabbing the contents of the trays with eye watering speed as you are being mugged by a crack FOMO expert, who is reaching for their prized possessions over the top of you (i.e., fear of missing out person).

While you are re-dressing and putting all the stuff back in some sort of order, apparently you are looking and acting suspicious because the

oOo

contents that had fitted into the bag before has now expanded, and what you are not clamping between your knees is all over the floor. Somehow, now the bag has shrunk. I feel it is due to the sub-zero customer service officer's attitudes, because they hate you.

Waving a cattle prod in your direction you are asked to step aside and pull it all out again while being scanned with a metal detector in case you are smuggling something mysterious in your bra. Don't laugh, it happens to us bigger girls.

Up next is the Conga line through Immigration, as you endure the moaning impatient prat behind you with their ankle breaking armour-plated carry-on bag, trying with gusto to propel you forward. It is because clearly you have only moved one 'poofteenth' of an inch instead of two, therefore hindering their progress in the queue. I understand their plight, as probably they are as wide eyed and bushy tailed as I am to get to Duty-Free to be sprayed with at least eight to ten types of perfumes by those cardboard cut-outs in uniforms with frozen in time doll like faces.

The Duty-Free obstacle course is like a ride on a Ghost Train with steely faced beings with heads like anvils, trained to jump out in front of you to dislodge your credit card at will. To which we succumb on most occasions, because by then you are just a shadow of your former self.

Finally flopping into a seat, surrounded by your carry-on wheelie thing, and a handbag with 5000 compartments, so you can't find anything without breaking a nail or dislocating a finger, your coat and neck pillow, and several bags of just in case duty free, you take a breath.

After hyperventilating for a few hours, a life-giving long breath and a very welcome sigh untangles you enough to take a little glance at the time-piece. Because another feeling is now taking residence and is saying that you are a bit peckish, as breakfast, if any, was hours ago, so

———————————— o0o ————————————

you do the walk. It's more like a stroll through the food court or a maze of eateries of things that all look unappealing and all look the same. So you settle for a triple bypass burger and a side of acid reflux.

Just as your eyelids start to weigh heavier than the descending burger, the announcement to board the plane billows out and you are awakened to the frenzied conga line on the move. FOMOS to the right and synchronized screaming kids to the left. Oh NO! In which of the 5000 hiding places did I put my Boarding Pass.

By this time your carry-on feels like you are dragging a building and your shoulder bag is precariously swinging between your aching neck and your throbbing bursa. Then you do the walk, but this time you are at a slightly abnormal angle so you don't remove someone's head on your way to your seat.

Within a split second of sitting in your seat and you are fumbling around to put stuff somewhere, within the confined space, you have to stand up to let an overzealous fat idiot in, to mark his territory in the seat next to you. Just your luck he is a twister, yes one of those guys that is constantly adjusting his landing gear, because now his undies are askew from all that twisting. One look at him and you immediately can tell that his undies may have seen better days as well.

We are strapped in and in the air, and you remember to breathe again and time to finally relax after the encounter with the frenzied air-heads less travelled, who are now fiercely poking at the on-board screen looking to be entertained immediately in case their heads cave in. I find that more entertaining than some of the movies.

Settling in nicely, you are then confronted with a coffin on wheels being manoeuvred down the passageway by a smile on a stick, "Something to drink ma'am?" followed by "The chicken or the fish?".

That is a hard decision as you are still trying to digest the murder burger, which seems like only a short time ago it was consumed. On inspection of the contents on the tray that has been thrust at you, the decision to eat it is driven by the fear that it is a long time before touchdown. Judging by the feeding frenzy going on around you, you figure, well it must be ok and you had better hurry up as they are coming by with that metal mickey contraption to collect the trays.

Within a "nano" second of the feeding frenzy being over the flying twisting idiot beside you has thrust the seat back and is making a few last adjustments, and with the landing gear safely tucked away he falls instantly into a deep coma. Peace at last you muse, as the cabin lights dim and you slowly start to drift as it has been a heck of a day so far.

The hum of the plane is suddenly shattered by the now flying, snoring idiot beside you. I swear this dude has lungs like a Navy Seal, he could free dive for what seems like several record-breaking minutes. Every half hour the Steward has to pull the dividing drapes out of his nostrils, for the privacy of the other passengers.

You do your best to sleep, after several hours in the air, but your swollen legs and ankles are quite painful from being immobile. The now fermenting stodge from earlier is letting its trapped presence known. The very thought of disturbing the time bomb sleeping next to you, prevents you from endlessly searching through the handbag maze, to look for the acid relief you thought you had packed with the step ladder in your handbag.

Next best thing is to join the queue to the Water Closet, with the hope that you will get some relief. Well, it helps a little, but looking on the bright side it is an opportunity as you are waiting, to take a refreshing look around at fellow bubbling and gurgling digestive tracts around you. Oh well, that little stretch and a yawn was enough to prompt you to

—————————————————— o0o ——————————————————

try and attempt to have a little snooze to last you until the descent into civilization.

Well good luck with that, as there are a few hundred forward thinking bladders and colons that have built up enough pressure to blow off both legs making their pilgrimage to the WC. In my personal opinion, all long distant aircraft should be fitted with a trough like a sheep dip, because by this time in the air your normal senses are returning after the asphyxiation from the crop dusters in the Perfume Department. The fragrant high notes have diminished, and if you have an aisle seat, which you were pretty smug about starting off, now exposes you to the passing parade of cabin crotch.

That's enough to give anyone a headache which is daunting knowing that after you land, the process of lining up to disembark is bitter-sweet, as you drag your bloated body to line up to go through immigration, then line up to retrieve your swaying mammoths, amidst the human shield of FOMOs, then line up to exit through customs. By this time, you have forgotten why you are there and you have lost the will to live.

Isn't it funny, when you reach your destination all you want to do is sit down, nothing is functioning, it seems that any memory of movement is gone. That feeling can last for several days, but you know you are alive by the aches and pains that have moved to another location in your body. Some people call it jet lag, I call it pay back! Your body is threatening you with extinction if you ever do that again.

—————————————————————— oOo ——————————————————————

10 Steps for Easy and Comfortable Travelling

1. Plan ahead to reduce stress. Make a checklist. Get plenty of sleep and rest before traveling. Recommend Mae-Rose Essential Sleep oil to help you relax and or sleep while travelling.

2. Do some mild stretching exercises and, walking in between packing and planning. I highly recommend having some decompression treatment with a reputable Chiropractor to maintain the maximum amount of flexibility before and after travel.

3. Wear comfortable shoes and clothing. Ladies throw in a shawl or big scarf as they have a thousand and one uses. A pair of socks come in handy as well and don't take up much room.

4. Reduce the amount of sugar intake a few days before travelling. Drink several glasses of filtered water.

5. Have a Colon cleanse of your choice. i.e., Herbal laxative or a vegetable juice day.

6. Prepare and take healthier snacks with you, to avoid junk food. Eat before you leave home if possible or prepare a protein 'smoothie' to have along the way.

7. Sample Perfumes on a card, do not spray them on your skin. They may contain chemicals that your body will absorb.

8. Be selective with in flight foods, it is not compulsory to eat everything. Avoid eating desserts after a meal as the sugars are quicker to break down in your gut, and it sits on top of

—————————— o0o ——————————

other heavier food and ferments and, are guaranteed headache material.

9. In flight, take a half teaspoon of "Superior Soda" in water instead of carbonated drinks, to keep your body alkaline and avoid a build-up of painful gas. It is a Pharmaceutical Grade Bicarb, it also boasts some amazing attributes such as Aluminium free, Gluten free, Cholesterol free, Lactose free and Sugar free.

All Bicarbs are not the same, Superior Soda is the highest possible quality on the market. Also, a wonderful remedy before and after travelling to bathe in or soak your feet. email me for further info at endresults1@gmail.com

10. Carry some Essential Oils to assist anxiety or to sleep on long flights as they are the most potent form of herbal energy. They are also antiseptic and immune system stimulants. Also are excellent for daily first aid needs including coughs, colds, bites and stings. www.MaeRoseEssentials.com

11. If you choose to wear a face mask, I can recommend a Herbal Infused product for extra protection. Infused with Melaleuca Alternifolia Leaf Essential Oil.

12. Enjoy a movie, read a book or do a crossword puzzle for a while. Take the opportunity to relax, do the exercises on the flight chart to assist circulation. Then cover your eyes, do some deep slow breathing check in with your goals and dreams or make some new ones. You never know you might get lucky and fall asleep and before you know it you will be preparing to land.

This simple routine may seem like a sacrifice to some people, but it is less than a day to experience travelling in a more comfortable and enjoyable state. Jet lag is mostly your body trying to cope after the beating you put it through, and then we have the hide to blame old age.

www.MaeRoseMethods.com

— o0o —

CHAPTER 8

Staying Fit and Healthy at Any Age

CHAPTER 8

Staying Fit and Healthy at Any Age

> ❝
>
> *"The Ultimate Guide to Staying Active and Healthy for Seniors -*
> *Without a Gym"*

When we hear the words fit, healthy, active, and fun in one sentence, we immediately think: "How does that work?" It sounds like hard work with no fun to me. The mere thought of stuffing all those saggy bits into a garment that looks like a cling wrap tube, then lining up at the gym is enough to make you want to take a dive.

Strobing visions of Doris Whitegoods pumping iron and Nellie No Neck doing chin ups is as equally funny as being on a treadmill next to Lawrence of Arrhythmia, with Hopeful Harry bringing up the rear trying to balance on one of those big balls.

Speaking of the gym instructor, the guy that looks like a refrigerator with a head and arms like hospital wings, he is smugly trying to get you to develop muscles that you are never going to use. He struts around spitting out numbers between one and four with three repetitions, and he has not even noticed that we have passed out at number one, because he is looking at himself at all angles in the mirror.

He need not be so cocky as he has to strut around because his overdeveloped thighs prevent him from sitting down and he can't cross his legs for nuts and looks like he is carrying two sheep under his arms.

All jokes aside, I would love to show you a better way with some quick and simple ways to stay happy, healthy, fit and have loads of fun and energy.

Tip number one is, stay away from the beautiful peoples' gym.

Tip number two, tear up your yearly subscription to the shrink.

Tip number three, if you are digging a tunnel to get away from your low self-image, stop digging.

Tip number four, if you are visible from a space station, breathe in.

Tip number five, if you have no energy and you have to stand twice to make a shadow, take it slowly.

Tip number six, if you have to run around in the shower to get wet, eat some protein.

Tip number seven, if your body is like a stocking full of walnuts, don't move.

Tip number eight, the handle on your recliner does count as an exercise machine, rest.

Tip number nine, start your exercise program slowly, do a drive past.

Did I say all jokes aside? Well, I was just kidding.

Tip number ten, if you don't want to have fun and you can't take a joke, GO HOME.

"So what fits your busy schedule better, exercising one hour a day or being dead 24 hours a day?".

-o0o-

———————————————— o0o ————————————————

That list is just a deterrent to make you stop and think if you are unfit or have not exercised in a while; it is better to have a laugh than a heart attack. A large number of unnecessary deaths occur when people get a sudden whim to get fit and then "the fit hits the shan, if you will pardon the pun, because a body can go into shock and has no reserve to recover. Take a sensible approach so you can live to enjoy it, by attending a gym with specialist trainers for seniors. (NB the above intended pun is a play on words and more polite than saying when "the shit hits the fan")

Yes, set aside one hour a day to start a practical health and fitness regime. Just walk thirty minutes in one direction and thirty minutes back. As you get stronger just increase the speed but stay within the hour. If you are a swimmer add that in as well. As we are rear wheel drives, moving the thighs has the best impact to increase overall fitness, as they are the biggest bones and muscles in the body.

The thighs are connected to the hip bones (I can hear you singing the rest.) The hips cradle the base of the spine that harbours the spinal cord that is connected to the head. If you look at the vertebral column system you will note that there is a series of small bones with cushions in between that allow us to move and be flexible. It is designed for movement and each compartment has a rhythm.

The human body is mysteriously and wonderfully made. There is detail behind the detail and science is still learning from it. The more I learned from Cranial-Sacral and Polarity Therapy the more fascinated I became with how our wireless anatomy works from built-in instructions that began with the inception of the human race that starts to grow immediately upon conception.

Walking therefore moves the pelvis forward and the head goes backwards and your diaphragm acts like a fulcrum, liken it to a see saw action that acts like a pump creating a negative/positive action which is movement. Therefore, improving circulation and elimination that allows for effective digestion; a high performing digestion involves better absorption and assimilation. It is the most cost-effective way to start a living younger longer process, and it's free.

Walking for seniors is the safest and healthiest way to start a health and fitness regime.

We are so blessed living in the city of the Gold Coast as our local Council has provided safe and comfortable walking trails amongst the most incredible scenic backdrops in the world. The boardwalks around the northern lakes take you up close and personal with grazing kangaroos as you stroll through natural bushland.

The rain forest walks in the nearby mountains provide the opportunity to share in the natural beauty and some of the oldest lofty trees in the world. Enjoy spectacular ferns and crisp clean mountain air while enjoying the sounds of the forest bird life. The views from the mountain roads and lookouts will take your breath away as you gaze at the majestic waterfalls and the rock pools. The choice of vistas is varied: you can sit in a restaurant and dine either looking at the valleys to the west or take in a spectacular portrait of the ocean in the far distance proudly displaying the city in all its glory.

It is possible to walk along the shoreline for hours on beaches that never seem to end as you take in health giving negative ions from the sea. The incredible pathways winding around the headlands are always full of surprises especially when migrating whales or dolphins are putting on a show.

Our beautiful Botanic Gardens have something for everyone, especially the scenic walking trails, and garden areas where you can read or write. I found inspiration for some of the contents of this book just by taking in the ambience.

---------------------------------- oOo ----------------------------------

I could write a book on my home town, in fact I am, because there is too much to do, see and enjoy including the amazing walks which I have only touched on. Apart from being a photographer's paradise, and one of the most sought-after tourist destinations in the country, it is home to many well-known celebrities whom you may come across as you are out walking.

Take the time and the advantage of these stunning areas in your city or town, to be grounded and unwind. Sometimes our sensory systems are stirred by sight, sound, taste and smell, nature provides all of this service for free.

-o0o-

You are unique. Discovering what gives your life meaning is one of the most important personal goals that you can pursue. You and your emotional well-being are inseparable partners in this adventure called life. Many people spend most of their life conforming to the expectations of others rather than focusing on their own feelings, goals, and aspirations, so that core contentment escapes them. There is a great deal of research that supports the concept that greater meaning in your life comes from having more personal fulfilment. There is no official formula for achieving lasting fulfilment as a senior, as everyone's goals and values are unique. However, here are a few topics that may be helpful to consider as you strive for fulfilment in your later years.

Reflecting on your life's purpose, ask yourself, "What are your values and goals and how would you like to make a difference in your world around you?" Give some serious consideration to what gives your life meaning and how you can align your actions with those values.

Engage in activities that bring you joy and satisfaction. Find hobbies and activities that bring you happiness and a sense of accomplishment.

This could be anything from volunteering and helping others to pursue a creative passion or learning new skills.

To do and achieve anything you must take care of your physical and mental health; this can make you feel at your best and enjoy life to the fullest.

This may involve eating a healthy diet, exercising regularly and seeking help for any mental health concerns which will lead to your overall happiness. But don't underestimate the power of short-term happiness and good and positive thoughts to influence the course of your mental health over the longer term. Get to know the source of anxieties and stresses to get rid of learned limiting beliefs that have become habits that seem normal.

Develop good thoughts and feelings that lead to better and productive habits that will result in long-term results which in turn reward you with excellent health. As for the bigger problems or challenges, mindfulness is a way to see them more clearly for what they are. As you get better at turning into your subconscious mind, you will start to see patterns. I found for example, that my mind was mulling over and worrying about all the possible choices in decisions that weren't made. It caused me endless unnecessary stress.

Once I saw this clearly, and finally recognised how destructive this habit of indecisiveness was, it showed that I had to change. I started making decisions more quickly, just to try a new way. Immediately experienced how stress diminishes once a decision was made. My habits and productivity began to change and I was getting more done with less to no anxiety.

The most basic mindfulness exercise is to just sit quietly and start paying attention to everything going on in your body and mind. Of course, this can be difficult if you have never done it.

—————————————— oOo ——————————————

Staying fit and healthy is easy once you are fit and healthy, but if you are not, that is another story. We have been told that our problems are age related and we will need drugs or surgery to fix it, or worse still, live with it. Sadly, that is the educated guesses of the medical profession and we are not to question it.

When we are desperate with no answers, we are tempted to go off to some bell ringing, mumbling anaemic "Twonk", who insists that navel gazing while removing the fluff will heal anything including death. If we were to take this as gospel, we would all be screwed as with most of us who are in our prime have self-cleaning navels, so contemplating our navel seems a bit naff.

These little "National Treasures" have hypnotic voices like asthma put to music. They have a way of convincing you that if you do some of their rituals and drink a potion that looks and tastes like industrial grey water, you will be back to your OLD self in no time.

I suggest you pay "madam magic" in rabbit skins and run. However, on the way out gently inform her that you don't want to go back to your old self, as that is not what you were there for, instead you are in hot pursuit of your NEW self. You never know you may pass on to her an interesting point of view worth thinking about.

❝

"There is no secret sauce for sizzling health, and aging, there is a source that is not a secret, it's just hidden behind a dream"

- Mae-Rose

oOo

So get off your assets, think and grow into a buoyant healthy body and mind. You don't need to be medicated all of the time. Your body knew how to heal itself before you came along: find out what it really needs. We don't get headaches because we have a lack of Aspirin. Use your waning logic - it makes more sense to take out the insults we put in the Temple in the first place.

Stress, anxiety, panic, envy, jealousy, greed, anger...to name just a few insults, create cortisol (short explanation: it is a self-created toxin equivalent to Napalm in the body). You can shovel all the vitamins, minerals, organic everything in and wave some feathers about and listen to some Dolphins singing. For all the good it does, you may as well have a couple of beers and eat a horse between two mattresses, don't stress just eat it, bless it, and send it on its way.

I am not saying that all of the above does not work; it does, in the right environment and in the right way. Cortisol becomes like a narcotic and destroys the body's ability to digest, absorb and assimilate, so it is a waste of time and money. Then it brings on more stress because you think you are doing the right thing, and when you get very little or no results, you beat yourself up.

> **"**
>
> *"There is an old saying that if you stand on a cat's tail, it's the other end that yells"*
>
> - Mae-Rose

So deep wouldn't you agree? It's my version of Physics.

More to the point, you treat the source of the stress. Address the central nervous system, nurture it and it will look after you when you care about something bigger than you. It is a human differential engine; the small wheel will drive the big wheel when you seek out experience that releases Dopamine.

Dopamine (the happy hormone) is like marinating all of your cells in self-care and love, so seek out ways to increase your supply. Start with fun people and *"Hang your own wet blanket out to dry, un-pucker your misery, be fun and interesting to be with."*

> **"**
>
> *"Hang your own wet blanket out to dry, un-pucker your misery, be fun and interesting to be with"*
>
> - Mae-Rose

Learn to laugh… Laughing helps relieve depression, pain and anxiety. It stimulates yet it relaxes, it gives every organ in the body a good workout, and it's fun. Learn to laugh heartily every day.

> **"**
>
> *"I intend to live forever, or die trying, in the meantime I'm staying more than alive"*
>
> - Mae-Rose

SMILE

Smiling is infectious, you catch it like the flu,

When someone smiled at me today, I started smiling too,

I passed around the corner, and someone saw my grin,

When he smiled back at me, I realised I'd passed it onto him;

I thought about that smile then I realised it's worth,

A single smile, just like mine could travel around the earth,

So if you see a smile begin, don't leave it undetected,

Let's start an epidemic quick, and get the world infected.

- Spike Milligan

-o0o-

www.MaeRoseMethods.com

CHAPTER 9

Aging With a Smile

CHAPTER 9

Aging With a Smile

"

"How to Embrace the Funny Side of Growing Older"

Successful Seniors Life Shopping Catalogue - Latest Edition.

A Lift Out Guide for Quick and Simple Ways to Stay Happy, Healthy, Fit and Have Loads of Fun and Energy:

Get a free gift with every self-order, it's toll free and delivered to your door.

1. Go anywhere Lumber support… Stop bending over backwards.

2. Senior fitness in two easy steps… Stop running up hills and running down people.

3. Easy way to maintain gum health… Stop flapping them.

4. Stop searching for answers... Be your own remote control.

5. How to enjoy your comfort zone… Make it stylish.

6. No buttons, No fuss life… Just play.

7. Quick and easy gadget to open a stubborn mind… A number Nine Boot.

---

o0o

8. Autopilot not working… Clear the Runway.

9. Become Cordless and Portable… Unplug from idiots.

10. Hearing Problems, never want to miss another word… Shut up and listen.

11. How to keep your dignity within reach… Mind your own business.

12. Light your way to dim areas… Light up someone's day.

13. Want more space… Clear out the shed in the backyard of your mind.

14. Want to be inspired… Spiral within.

15. Effortlessly unscrew bad behaviour… Get out of your own way.

16. Draw out toxic thinking… Read a good book.

17. How to clean hard to reach places in your mind… Write a book.

18. Reach and Wipe without harmful twisting… Use your imagination.

19. Prevent friction… Rearrange your mental deck chairs.

20. How to have younger looking thoughts… Open a new can of Friends.

21. Help to reduce pain… Change the way you think.

22. Gain extra grip on Life… Let go of BS.

23. Help relieve sore and stiff attitudes… Get a Sensa Huma.

24. Want discreet protection… Sit on it.

25. See things Bigger and Clearer... Use your inner magnifying glass.

26. Avoid sore and aching Legs... Stop jumping to conclusions.

27. If one door closes and another one opens... You need a Tradie.

28. Transform a dull corner... Get a life.

29. If your Life seems short... Smile while you have got teeth.

30. Stiff Neck and Shoulders... Stop holding up the world.

31. Want unsightly features out of sight... Try an easy to assemble Attitude.

❝

Thank you for shopping *"Successful Seniors"*

- Mae-Rose

-o0o-

When you have more past than future and your life flashes before your eyes as you experience your first slip over in the shower antic and you have to wait several seconds before you can walk, you know you need handles. Suddenly you feel the need to think two weeks in advance when going anywhere to check if there are sufficient knobs, rails and handles.

Some mornings you wake up already injured and your leg has gone to sleep, you know the rotten thing is going to be awake all night. So you think ahead and plan where you can find a parking spot for your knees and you can sit like you are about to play the Cello till relief arrives.

---

o0o

AH! It is a good time while sitting to reminisce about the days you could defy the laws of gravity and take your bra off without getting undressed. Happiness then was getting that thing off after a hard day's work, and having a good scratch.

Now is a different story…isn't it girls? With the fingers being a bit numb and you are about to hook up…it takes off away from your body like a catapult. What about when you try and retrieve the mongrel thing and you stretch it out to get more traction and the other end goes mental; it is like conquering the art of using Japanese Nunchucks while rhythmically dislocating your shoulders.

You boys never had to put up with that nonsense, you never missed a beat, always famous for doing three things all at once, you could leap, fart and whistle. You can still multi-task and do three things at once, the dynamics may have changed but nevertheless you can bend over, do up your shoes, while managing to breathe.

We may have traded our midriffs for wisdom, but we have gained the fun of managing our staircase wit, having the ability to turn 10 minutes of entertainment crammed into an hour just by opening a packet of crisps. Who needs a Rubik's cube when you can fill in a good half hour extracting those little plastic caps with mini rings on the top of sauce bottles. Especially when they snap off. Who you gonna call?

Is it just me or does someone get into your wardrobe, without attracting observation, and perform some covert operation and surreptitiously overlap your coat hangers. When you go to get a garment out to wear it is like cracking open a Bank Safe; those babies are immovable, so your only option is run to the shed for a blow torch.

By this time, you have become so angry and frustrated you could back a caravan with your bare hands. With a set to your jaw and one foot on the door frame you give one ferocious pull and some colourful threats,

o0o

and before you know it you become a Wing Commander and are flying backwards across a crowded room. If the undignified landing wasn't humiliating enough, your view from the floor reveals you are holding a hanger without a hook, as the hook is still on the rail and your coat is nowhere to be seen.

My favourite is re-finding the elusive hole in the onion bag. I swear there is a nasty little onion bag gnome sitting in the basket waiting for me to turn my back. I have sat there on a chair pulling all-nighters, with my double barrel shotgun across my lap, to no avail. It must have some special kind of invisible power in those rosy pontoon like cheeks, and with one puff can seal up the hole by remote control.

What sadistic individual invented Band-Aids, especially "one type fits all". What about us? Personally, I believe it's a deliberate attempt to drive us into the abyss. The packet they come in has an invisible tab that only a hawk could see, but dead easy for the person who comes to your rescue. You simply can't ask them to locate the opening of the wafer-thin bits at the end to expose the actual Band-Aid, so you blow on it and watch for the slightest movement.

Ah Ha! You bring on your Bruce Lee and rip the wrapper off, but your triumph takes a downward turn as you face the task of removing the cover off the sticky bits. Those evil little so and so's see you coming and turn in on themselves and lie there laughing while you repeat the process over and over or watch you bleed to death.

Creative overlaps in our dialogue are now required, according to some follically challenged do-gooder, because apparently having afternoon tea and dipping Ginger Nuts into hot tea is now called bullying. More tea Vicar?

Still if you have got a bit of residual dignity left that you would like to get rid of, have some fun with these tips. If you are expecting a visit from

—— oOo ——

a family that looks like they are from the department of live-stock and freshwater fish, with smoke lines from whistling too much Dixie, or the Gargoyles from next door pop over to satisfy their galloping curiosity about the strange car in the driveway, answer the door with your pants on back to front and inside out, with a "Who said I had a weekend" look on your face.

If that does not get rid of them without a fight, leave a few incontinence pads casually lying about and slightly dampen the chairs. Drag about with a meter of toilet paper on the bottom of your shoe, don't flush the loo, leave a little surprise in there. Keep it up until you smell fear, as the mere hint of responsibility will get rid of them.

"

"If you lose one sense, your other senses are enhanced. People with no sense of humour have an increased sense of self-importance"

- Unknown

www.MaeRoseMethods.com

CHAPTER 10

Dinosaurs never die, they just become Authors

CHAPTER 10

Dinosaurs never die, they just become Authors

> **"**
>
> *"Wise people speak because they have something to say; fools talk because they have to say something"* - Plato

What Other Seniors Do to Live Life to The Fullest

What do you get when you put an old introverted dried arrangement into a room full of bright young flowers, all in pursuit of becoming budding authors? Have you seen these animated stampeding strangers who are quick to answer because they have all the answers, and they are the loudest in the room. They are so pumped and puffed up and over the top and so eager to pose questions, because they are full of ideas, and God forbid and they are all herded together in a room?

I'll tell you what you get, it's Liquid Fear! Sitting in your own body fluids in a paralysed state is enough to take the sting out of death. All you want to do is run out the door and lie face down in the nearest Fiord or jump in the sea and pull a wave over your head.

My big ideas of expanding on the little bit of writing experience I had soon turned into terror at my first introductory class into the world of literature. When the screaming, clapping, wired host took a breath and the loud throbbing dance music died down, I slapped the side of my head and wondered if I had taken a wrong turn and ended up in a gym or in a size 10 to zero fashion boutique in the mall. That feeling of sheer misplacement took the lustre clean off my dreams like heavy duty paint stripper on an old rocking chair.

Oh NO! Once again, the Dinosaur of the class, I felt like I should have been in the hair up hem down class, with sensible shoes and a back brace. With a set to my jaw and flared nostrils, I said to myself, "Haven't you learnt your lesson yet?" This was not the first time I decided to build upon my education and enjoy learning and growing in the face of adversity.

I have always had a burning passion to learn and teach, to become more and share more. Alas, apparently, according to close family members at the time, who oddly enough had attitudes and faces like chain smoking Trout, sternly stated I should have been content to make sandwiches at the local Servo, or sit staring out the window like Whistler's Mother at my so-called age.

My drive and tenacity propelled me forward because I had a lot to give and a lot to say and express and I loved new challenges. Navigating my way through the minefields back then was depressing and frustrating if you weren't a star or have a degree. However, I did enjoy writing articles for Health and Fitness magazines, travel brochures, stage show and theatre reviews, and some editorials for Car Rally events. I was the go-to person to write Eulogies. Sadly, I did not put my name to anything for fear of judgement and ridicule.

I stayed buried in my work for a lot of years as a Natural Health therapist and Self Development facilitator assisting in the success and progress of others and loved it. Bit by bit I grew past the naysayers, and well-informed bigots and led them in the direction of a good Taxidermist.

---

o0o

I became passionate in bringing out the best in myself and others, instead of trying to fix them, and took a hard look at my level of tolerance. I kept reaching up to the next level and mixing with like-minded people who kindly encouraged me to look around and embellish the successes great and small that I had accomplished.

As therapists we understand the healing power of writing down your thoughts and fears and how encouraging it is to set your goals. However, we were never prepared for the dynamic impact on our lives writing a book can have.

When I joined Global Publishing Group I knew in my heart what I wanted to write about, but was hesitant about my topic when I learned of the fascinating and interesting content my fellow authors were writing about.

Once again, the Dinosaur syndrome kicked in and all the old familiar doubts flooded in and I was looking out the window for a Fiord in close proximity. My defeatist driver suddenly emerged from the back of the bus and temporarily took over as I questioned why anyone would want to read a book about a bunch of old coffin dodgers.

Fortunately, my amazing tutors saw my little act and pulled that runaway bus over and parked it. I followed their guidance to the letter and did some research on seniors wanting to be successful and those who are successful in many areas.

I was barely into my search for alive and active Super-Agers, when the good old faithful Reticular Activating System popped up like a Jack-in-the-box and pointed in all directions. I was stunned as I thought I was the only one within a country mile, I was mistaken as they are everywhere, the world is littered with them. "I say to myself what a wonderful world" and it is in such good hands, hearts and minds.

When reflecting on my list of respected and revered people I realised that it would take more than one book to show why I have so much admiration for these exceptional people. I am so much in awe. I will share who they are briefly and I encourage you to go deeper and be inspired by such impressive role models.

Firstly, I am driven to show off and showcase a gaggle of more than amazing Super-Agers, some are turning their lives around, some are adding to their lives, some are playing just for fun, and a couple of stragglers who can't play Bingo. I am honoured and excited they are throwing themselves into my on-line "Successful Seniors" wealth creation course. The youngest one is in her sixties, and the oldest one is in his nineties.

-o0o-

I have been drawn to this great lady for many years, Ita Buttrose, AC, OBE, is an Australian TV network chairperson, television and radio personality, author and former magazine editor, publishing executive and newspaper journalist. The most celebrated female journalist in Australian history. This wonderful person is 81 years and is getting more brilliant as time goes on.

Betul Mardin, 97 years, was a professor in Istanbul till she was 86. Journalist, program specialist and producer at the Turkish Radio and Television Corporation. A lady who loves to dance for health, stays positive, keeps up to date to keep her mind sharp, loves the cinema and the theatre, deems it necessary to be with young people and vice versa. Maintains a positive attitude and stays young at heart.

The extraordinary Eileen Kramer, proving that age is just a number at 108 years of age. This truly inspirational and creative person is a dancer, choreographer, writer, painter and beautiful. This magnificent Australian Icon has no plans to retire. Go Girl!

Phil Liggett, 79 years, MBE, commentator and journalist, the voice of cycling, and a voice like a gravy sandwich that will stay with me forever. He has covered and called The Tour de France since 1973, and is still doing so, plus is still behind the microphone at other professional world cycling events around the world.

——————————————— o0o ———————————————

Leah Purcell, AM, is an Aboriginal Australian film director, novelist, playwright, stage and film actress. At the young age of 52 has not even reached middle aged as yet, but I am in awe of her outstanding talent, and I feel sure Leah will be the teller of many senior stories to come past and present.

Clive James. Some of his best quotes: *"A life without fame can be a good life, but fame without a life is no life at all"*. *"Fiction is life with the dull bits left out"*. *"All I can do is turn a phrase until it catches the light"*. This Australian critic, journalist, broadcaster, writer and lyricist captured my full attention with his ability to make language so pliable and picturesque. He instilled in me a love for the written and spoken word. He still lives in my memory with his famous "Premature Punctuation" sadly he died at the age of 80.

There is nothing like a Dame, why stop at one? Emma Thompson, Judi Dench, Maggie Smith, Helen Mirren, Julie Andrews, Shirley Bassey and myself although not yet a Dame. elen M At the time when I was researching and, writing this article I added all of our ages together and collectively, we rack up approximately 570 years of wow, wisdom and wonder.

Yes, they are all famous celebrities from stage and screen. I admire and respect this bevy of incredibly talented women because off-stage they are real and normal women defying the expectations of old age.

Who could possibly not put Richard Branson on their list. He is the epitome of success on so many levels. *"Do not be embarrassed by your failures, learn from them and start again"* is one of his famous quotes. He said in space *"To all you kids down there, I was once a child with a dream looking up to the stars"*. At 72 he is just hovering around middle age.

oOo

David Attenborough at an incredible 92 years. A natural historian and one of the most famous on the list of success seniors. There is so much to be said about his love and passion for nature.

The old saying that age is just a number was considered for many years a state of mind. To me and seniors I have interviewed, it is much more than that. It is an indication of success at excelling AT life despite their age. It is also a collection of experiences and projects, experiments and trials, a measurement of values and an accumulation of love and wisdom.

Spend a few rewarding hours researching the many wonderful and successful seniors past and present, their stories will give you inspiration, motivation, hope and reassurance that the best is yet to come.

“

” The young have many wishes, the old have only one”

- Mae-Rose

-o0o-

“

“True teachers use themselves as bridges, over which they invite their students to cross. Having facilitated that crossing, they joyfully collapse, encouraging them to make bridges of their own”

- Ancient Proverb

o0o

Mentors and Munters

There are no isolates in nature, so you don't have to do it alone. Having a coach and a mentor is beneficial, comforting and reassuring.

The investment you have made in yourself up to now is not just another wild goose chase. Wisely choose ones who are accountable to you and themselves and they are governed by integrity, knowing that it is within their interests to assist you in reaching your goals and positive outcomes.

They must aim for the optimum in accurate knowledge of your cause for their own credibility. A good coach will listen and ask what you want from the field they are coaching you in. An honest coach will ask you who your mentors are so they can get a clear understanding of what lights you up, and brings out the best in you.

A mentor, according to several dictionaries, is an experienced and trusted adviser who guides another to greater success. They are experts in their field, an authority to teach and give help to a lesser experienced person. Research points out that even very successful people have mentors, and they themselves attribute a lot of their success to the people they look up to.

Some have stated that not all of their mentors were famous, as their parents, grandparents or teachers may have had the greatest influence on them.

A great number of mentors who I hold in high esteem were refugees or their descendants who emerged as humanitarians and became leading doctors, surgeons, nurses, scientists, inventors, artists, social workers and so on. The list is endless.

They became trail blazers in their fields throughout history and have gained our respect because they are humble and do not encourage us to

—————————————————— o0o ——————————————————

idolise them because of their knowledge, experience and wisdom. Learn from these people and become teachable so that you can be an influencer with integrity and compassion for those in need.

The word "Munter", according to the dictionary, is an ugly person, a drunk person, or both. It was originally slang from English-speaking countries and turned it into some pretty colourful intonations. I have used the term to describe unethical people who pose as mentors, whose sole purpose is to take your money and steal your valuable time. They are drunk on their own self-importance and their ugly egos allow them to prey on your vulnerability.

In my own experience I have walked away from seminars, have signed up for deals and offers that have just left me with despair, which were a costly experience financially and time wise as well. I asked myself, "Is it me?" I had to give myself an honest answer, which was, "yes and no", as in my case it was a rude and unexpected awakening that I had to have. I went in with blind faith and ignorance, never questioned anything, I just assumed that this industry was about helping and educating.

Not to dwell on the negative, but some people are not remotely like mentors. Some are relying on you being gullible and vulnerable, and I suspect, nor do they care that you are not receiving a return on your investment in their course or deal.

Self-development and self-improvement have become a growth industry worth millions. In some cases, it is an idea packaged in tempting lures that give false hope. The name alone implies that there is something wrong with you, that you can't progress or achieve without their product, and that also will only work in the future.

The point of this little outburst is to help you ask the right questions and check if they are going to deliver everything they claim as they may be marketers and not teachers.

——————————————— o0o ———————————————

The lesson I want to share with you from the heart is I thank them for making it very clear to me the difference. They have given me the most valuable lesson of achieving clarity out of chaos. Now I can discern and choose the way I conduct myself as a woman, as a leader, as a mentor.

This will also be more helpful when you understand one of the major influences that shape the person who you want to be, and it must be understood that it is your association with others, the people you allow into your life. Never misunderstand the influences of those around you. It is so powerful, so subtle and so gradual that we often don't even realise how it can affect us. Be on guard, and be sure that your present associations are mentoring you to grow in the direction of your goals and dreams.

Are you becoming, achieving and acquiring what you want? Or are you letting "Munters" steal your dreams? If you are not sure, head for the centre of the pack of positive and progressive people. Look for people of substance and principles. People who accomplish great things through discipline, perseverance and honesty. Follow successful people to guide you to your success plan. Most successful people love to share their knowledge with others because they seek out those they admire.

> *"Association is a strategy for wealth, and happiness. Keep the weeds of negative influence from your life. Instead, 'farm' the seeds of constructive influence. You will not believe the harvest of good fortune you will reap"*
>
> - Jim Rohn

www.MaeRoseMethods.com

oOo

CHAPTER 11

How to Gain Vital High End
Financial Guidance and Advice
from Experts

CHAPTER 11

How to Gain Vital High End Financial Guidance and Advice from Experts

Now you have a clear view and are thinking from your future. You've had a bit of fun sorting yourself out and your prosperity path is set in place and it's time to get serious about your well-designed fortune.

All our lives we have been advised to work hard, save our money, buy a house, buy property or invest and sweat over our superannuation to come. So we squirreled away money in the bank like we were told to do and keep working hard till it was time to retire. By then you may have been affluent enough to pay off your three bricks in the suburbs, or you would win the pot at the end of the rainbow and manage not to snuff it in the meantime.

Yes, we, as in my family, did all of the above, until along the way we were presented with an investment opportunity that made sense. We had been working and saving, saving and working with monotonous regularity. Watching our parents and most other people around us slave their guts out for years, and get nowhere in particular. Hearing some rumblings in the background, we looked into various ways to increase our wealth, as we were developing a more strategic way of thinking.

Well, that was an odd use of the word thinking, more like blind faith as we took the advice of our lawyers, who dangled a very organic carrot under our green noses. All nodding in agreement around the impeccable oblong boardroom table, we pushed the tray of empty coffee cups aside to eagerly sign on the dotted line of each piece of paper in the mound of impressive legal documents.

---
oOo

Thinking that size does matter, we thought that the bigger the stack of papers, the better the size of the fortune, so we followed the hypnotic bouncing ball and our spinning egos and signed away like a herd of Baa Baa's.

All we had to do next was open the wallet take out a few dollars, and then slide them across the shiny table to be scooped up and put into the safe. We would perform that little ritual whenever we had a windfall or the mattress could not hold any more.

It became like a game, we even called dollars "slides" because we have a sense of humour and like a bit of fun, plus it seemed less painful while handing over our cash.

On their convincing sound advice over a period of time, we willingly transferred lump sums of hard-earned dollars out of our bank accounts, and into our so-called nest egg, as we were receiving dividends far better than the next to nothing microbial interest we were getting from the banks.

We would ride off into the sunset thinking we were hot shots because we were onto something cool and now, we had more time on our hands to go ball hunting; others may call this pastime Golf. As I like to call it, a form of attention deficit disorder: focus for twenty seconds and then walk for five minutes to look for frogs.

Nevertheless, we were feeling pretty smug that finally we had broken the family curse of scarcity consciousness. Not knowing much about red flags, because that was a different sport, we never thought to ask any questions about the dollar or slide holders {unmarked white envelopes} containing so-called dividends we received each month. It never occurred to us to question their methods because they were Lawyers.

Our parked dollars were being lent out to borrowers who paid back with nice interest, which we were told was absolutely legal and we believed

---

oOo

---

that the Solicitor Gods knew more than us small town hicks, so why question people we had known for years.

How important we felt when invited to the board room again on another, of what we thought, was another auspicious occasion. We sat there with a view of the fabulous stretch of water across the road from the building we were in, and gazed at the picturesque Island beyond, listening to the birds and the laughter of children in the park, with the sea breeze dancing through the open sliding doors on the third floor. Now why wouldn't that ambience put you in the mood to enjoy a glass of Chateau Nerang Embankment from the bottle shop next door, to discuss the next step on our way to becoming billionaires.

Not batting an eyelid, we excitedly agreed to add to our impressive regimes and now become conservationists and save the trees and do away with the white envelopes. This meant we rolled the dividends back into the coffers and accumulated more wealth. Happy as.

When our hats did not fit anymore because our heads had gotten bigger, we thought we would become land barons and invest in property, fittingly went to the office to shake the money tree, but the doors were locked and the phones weren't answered.

To make a long story short, seven figures later we, Baaasil, Beeeryl and Bruuuce, along with a large number of other Baa Baa's, became instant "inconvenienced" billionaires.

The moral to that short version of the story is, when it comes to your money, check and double check and then check again from different establishments. Ignorance is costly, so is blind faith, but worst still is assumed trust. Just because you see an impressive monogrammed business card and a Lloyd's of London look alike shingle over a door does not mean that your money is safe.

———————————————— o0o ————————————————

Gone are the days where you could leave the front door key under the pot plant or leave the doors in your house wide open while you go to the shop, or leave your car unlocked. Gone are the days when you could trust your lawyer. I would like to disclaim that I adamantly don't believe all lawyers and solicitors are corrupt. However, in my experience and research there are a few. My suggestion is to be on guard with everything.

-o0o-

Now that you have decided to accumulate more wealth with the extra twenty to thirty more years on top of what you have now, it is time to accumulate more knowledge to protect your legacy. In spite of my extremely shattering experience, I decided to make my loss a temporary situation and start all over again.

With the help of many people who have experienced similar issues I have made it my passion to get accurate answers to my questions to pass on to you to safeguard your assets and your estates and legacies.

In a discussion with my incredibly helpful publisher at the time of writing this book, I mentioned my desire to get some legal facts. I would like to share the lead up and the discussions that took place to help me make this happen as follows:

"Darren, many thanks for your welcome email and the opportunity to have an audience with the experts you have recommended. I am looking forward to gaining important relevant legal statistics to pass onto my readers.

I intend to dedicate a chapter in my book to create a step-by-step formula or road map for successful seniors, or those who are already successful, who may not have had a look at their situation for a while, and may need an update."

My questions are as follows:

1. The importance of having a will.

2. What is an executor and what type of executor is most suitable.

3. The role of a power of Attorney.

4. Is superannuation important?

5. Accountant or Bookkeeper or both.

6. Explain the difference between a Solicitor, Lawyer and Barrister.

7. Spreading assets.

The purpose of this list is to back-up and protect wealth creation and, in some cases, extra wealth creation, through books, courses and investments we, and others, have to offer. I do hope I have covered the relevant topics and will add anything that may come up. I am certainly open to your valuable input and experience.

Sincerely,

Mae-Rose

I had the absolute privilege of being introduced by Darren to a leading lawyer, head of Red Chip Law firm in Brisbane. Peter very kindly gave me an audience so that I could interview him and ask questions the average person does not know. It is very hard for people to know where to go, and to whom, for legal advice that is accurate. We tend to chat around the B-B-Q where most myths are created by a well-informed Uncle Fred and a carton of beer.

The legal system is very complicated and appears to us ordinaries to be written using three alphabets. There is no point in reading any documents, because we don't understand most of it, so it's beyond me why they ask us to read before we sign it, knowing full well that we will pretend so we don't appear a bit limp under the hat.

The first question I asked Peter was, "Is it important to have a will, and what is its purpose?"

It is very important to write a will, because it is a legal document that clearly outlines where and to whom your assets and goods and chattels are distributed after your death. Its purpose is to make sure your wishes are carried out by law under the supervision of a lawyer. A lawyer's role is to list in detail your requests regarding everything that you personally want to happen to your assets.

In the discussion the lawyer will draw out what actually has to be dealt with by identifying what your assets are and what issues need to be dealt with pertaining to those assets. Consulting with a lawyer who understands how estate planning works, like establishing if your assets are in a Trust, or a Company, or a Super Fund. This reveals the assets may not be yours.

Have your will written by a lawyer who will explain all of the details in simple terms prior to you signing. If there is something that you don't quite understand ask again. Because for some people it is an emotional occasion for various reasons, which may distort your understanding of the true meaning of the terms.

Lawyers are professional people but most also have a level of empathy and compassion, and they do understand your need for reassurance and clarity. After all they are human, and some time in their life they may be faced with the same issues.

It is not a huge financial outlay to pay to save your loved ones a lot of unnecessary stress and heartache while dealing with their emotion of your demise. In my research, particularly with the families I had interviewed, there is always one member of a family who is too proud or independent (or in some cases tight) who goes to the post office to get a

—————————— o0o ——————————

will kit. That is fine if your wishes and your estate is very straightforward and simple, it can, and has worked in so many cases.

On the other hand, as in my family, a relative with a sizable estate wrote his own will using a kit and lodged it with the Public Trustees. He clearly did not acquire or receive any legal advice, as there were several unclear instructions. The distribution of his assets was not distinctly marked and very vague.

When some distant cousins from the mountains turned up, I am sure you are familiar with this lot (the ones that had only visited him a few times in his whole life) got wind of this they came in with guns blazing and contested that they should be beneficiaries. We were also stunned when we received letters containing Affidavits from some greedy neighbours through their lawyers claiming that they were entitled as well.

The bottom line was that it took years with the fighting back and forth, and they won in the end, don't ask me how. By the time the lawyers were paid out for their services, the estate was reduced to less than half, and in a way, everyone lost except for a certain few.

In the event of your death and a will has not been written, it is another messy business. Peter explained that in Australia, each of the States have what is called a Succession Act.

This is a piece of legislation that governs all of the estates and wills that are left un-instructed, and this goes according to a set formula. If you have a spouse and or some children, the estate will be split, half to the spouse and then half to the children.

If you don't have a will, then whoever would be next in line to administer the estate, which might be a spouse, and then it might be the children. Who then has the right to apply to the court to step in and basically be the executor?

If you don't have a spouse or children then it goes to your parents and brothers and sisters still living or it works its way down the family tree.

The downside of this is that the estate can end up going to someone that you did not intend, like the cousins from the mountains who suddenly pop up over the herbaceous hedge, shouting mine, mine, mine.

The Succession Act has however clear guidelines about who can contest a Will, called Family Provision Claim, basically meaning you have got to be someone who is a child or a dependent. Often the courts take the view that if you're a child and have been overlooked they will look at it from a fair point of view and negotiate a share. The alternative is that The Public Trustee becomes the administrator of the estate, consequently that is where it lands if you don't have a list as there is nowhere else for it to go.

One of the options of The Public Trustees is to come in to act as an Executor of a Will, when one of your choice is not appointed.

An Executor, also known as a Personal Representative, also known as a Testator, is either a person or an institution that you personally choose and appoint to carry out the wishes of your Will. It is important to keep in mind that if you are selecting a person, you need to evaluate whether they are a reliable and responsible person and they are not necessarily emotionally involved, but to execute your wishes from a logical point of view.

Your Executor should be someone you can trust and who is capable of managing the responsibilities that come with that role. It is crucial that you discuss your wishes with your potential Executor beforehand and make sure they are willing to take on that task.

Some common choices of Executors include family members, friends or professionals such as lawyers or accountants.

It is a sensible idea to choose an alternate Executor in case the first choice is unable or has to decline. This will ensure that your wishes are still carried out even if your first choice is unable to serve as your Executor.

—————————————— oOo ——————————————

You can have more than one and they can act as a group and must be over the age of eighteen, as it is their job to see that your wishes are carried out exactly as you have stipulated in your last will and testament.

If you do not have anyone of that calibre, your legal representative may make a reference to a person or an institution that will be responsible.

Another important role is to have a Power of Attorney (POA) to grant authority to another person ["agent or attorney-in-fact"] to act on their behalf. The agent can be given broad or limited power, depending on the specific terms of the POA.

Their role is to allow the agent to make decisions and take actions on behalf of the principal person. This is very helpful in situations where a person is not able to make decisions for themselves due to illness, absence, or disability.

The following are some examples of some different types of POAs, each with different purposes and scopes of authority.

A healthcare or a medical decision may have to be made on behalf of a person who is unable to make it for themselves. That type of attorney is able to grant the agent permission to do so.

A legal power of attorney grants the agent the authority to make legal decisions on behalf of a person, like appearing in court or signing contracts.

A financial attorney grants the agent the authority to manage the person's financial affairs such as filing taxes, managing investments and paying general bills.

The agent must act in the best interests of the principal and in accordance with the terms of the POA. It is vital to know that a power of attorney can be revoked at any time as long as the person to whom the POA applies is mentally competent.

---

oOo

"Is superannuation important?" It is important for you, if you are employed because the whole idea around the superannuation regime is to encourage people to put money into a super fund to save money. The employer must put aside a percentage of gross salary into a superannuation fund. So the more you save the more you will have for the future. It is not a magic wealth creation facility, it's a toolbox, to utilise when you retire. Treat it like it's a money box that you can't take the money out of until you reach retirement age.

You can "retire" (stop working) whenever you like but the super cannot be accessed until you reach a government-set age. Some industries have lower age releases than others.

Super is a place to invest your money. It's your money, it stays your money, it's just locked in for a period of your working life as a safeguard. As an incentive to do that it pays less tax, and there is a lot of advantages to having part of your retirement financially secured in a superannuation fund.

Most financial planners would recommend that people save some money in super because of the tax benefit. You pay 15% tax as opposed to 30% tax up to a recently defined $3M total. This topic would be better taken to a financial planner to answer as they would be able to look at each person's particular circumstances.

My next question was, "Should we have a bookkeeper or an Accountant?" We both agreed that both have an important role, as many a business has gone broke just by not having proper records, even when the business appears to be doing well.

Again, it depends how big or small the business is, daily transactions should be recorded. Incomings and outgoings need to balance, and that takes time. Michael Gerber, author of "The E Myth" book series, explains why most small businesses don't work, and what to do about it. He does state that part of the dilemma is trying to do it all by yourself.

o0o

A small business can easily keep track by adopting good habits of keeping all records in one place, and keeping records daily. An accountant may be required to reconcile accounts for taxation purposes.

Large businesses or companies definitely need an accountant and perhaps a bookkeeper, for obvious reasons. In all cases an accountant who is also a financial planner is even a more beneficial option.

When you need to obtain legal advice, the average person like me is never sure where to start, especially where and with whom to approach for your particular circumstances. I posed the question to Peter to explain to me what the difference is between a Lawyer, a Solicitor and a Barrister.

I wanted to hear the right explanation from an actual legal person. As we have all been guilty of obtaining the wrong or misleading information around the B-B-Q.

Lawyer is a generic term that covers Solicitors and Barristers, like an umbrella that covers both. Although it is one legal profession, it has two strands - Barristers and Solicitors both have the same law degree, both get qualified in the same way. A Barrister has to do a particular course to qualify, in turn so does a Solicitor have to qualify in a particular course.

Barristers are mostly advocates and spend most of their time in court, as that is their area of focus and do not necessarily deal with the public. They rely on briefs given to them by Solicitors. They are advocates who present their clients' cases before courts and tribunals, known as the Bar, and provide legal opinions and advice.

A Solicitor is a legal practitioner who provides specialist advice on various issues, who deals traditionally with the public. For instance, even if you do go to a Barrister who deals in Succession Law, they are not the people to go to have your will written.

Is it wise to have all of your eggs in the one basket. Once again it depends on the size of your nest eggs. Also depends on what sort of assets you have. Our family lost savings, plus our transferred superannuation fund that had been cashed in. Fortunately, we still owned our home, so we did not hit rock bottom, but unfortunately some other investors lost everything.

Be sensible when it comes to making financial decisions, always think capital preservation first and seek professional advice with a financial planner/solicitor combined who will provide asset spreading solutions.

Do extensive research to gain as much knowledge as you can to avoid any loopholes that can bring financial ruin.

Please note that this is a very brief rundown on a huge but necessary subject. I merely wanted to make you aware of an area in your life that may have been pushed onto the back burner or under the carpet to await a rainy day. The information given is just a curtain raiser and may not be totally accurate, so please do due diligence on a part of your life that can make you or break you.

I am ever so grateful to Peter McLaughlin and his firm for giving their valuable time to give us some very profound and vital legal advice.

Contact Red Chip Law firm and book an appointment to ensure your affairs are in order. The contact details are listed in the Recommended Resource section of this book.

www.MaeRoseMethods.com

———————————————— o0o ————————————————

CHAPTER 12

Feathers and Sequences

CHAPTER 12

Feathers and Sequences

The importance of Strategies, Systems and Sequences

Those were the days! Back in the sixties, seventies and eighties when you came limping home at some ungodly hour of the morning, attempting to beat the milkman to the door. It seems really odd to say that now, but looking back, it was a great time to experience because it is a thing of the past that we will never see again. We lived remotely in a small country town with an Air Force base, meat works and woollen mills industry, with a substantial number of brickworks. The whole town and the outlying areas were the hub of a massive coal mining industry.

Let me break this down for you if by chance you happen to be on the younger side. It was a very industrial area; there were shops in the town, but for us that was miles away and we only drove in there once a week as Dad was the only driver. So our daily needs were delivered to our row of 12 houses that were built during World War II to house workers of the nearby pottery and brickworks.

I still have fond memories of the baker delivering our bread; it was not even wrapped let alone sliced, but it was still warm. We could not wait to cut a big fat slice off and hit it with an equal amount of home-made butter and thickly spread peanut butter, or mulberry jam made from our trees, or honey from Grandad's bees, and sometimes when Mum was not looking, all of them. Oh! Where was I? Well, if you think that is primitive, as a small child I remember the baker rode into our neck of the woods with a horse and cart and the bread was in a basket with a gingham cloth covering.

—————————————— o0o ——————————————

At that time the ice man delivered big blocks of ice as there was no refrigeration, so we had an ice chest that was big and heavy and sat on the floor. It had a separate compartment on the top that kept the bottom cold for the next day or two.

Also like most families back then we had a cabinet which for all the world looked like a bird cage and it was hung on a hook on the veranda. It kept the flies and insects out and allowed the air to circulate through.

We lived in a sub- tropical area so food was never stored for long because of the hot weather, plus we had the added benefit of having most of it there on the land. It was quite normal for us and we never went without. Now I stand in my kitchen and smile as I now have a fridge the size of a bungalow.

Some weeks we would get very busy and the greengrocer rattled in, driving a big red truck with running boards to stand on to choose your vegetables or fruit. We were very self-sufficient and grew several crops, one of them being peanuts. I had never seen peanut butter in a jar till I was a lot older as we always made our own. Sometimes we traded what we grew, always we seemed to have an over-supply of peas and corn along with trays of organic eggs from our chickens.

Once a week, Mr Burnell the pie man would supply Pie Floaters (a pie with mushy peas, gravy, and hot sauce) to the workers at the Pottery. Prior to that he would have driven through the many coalmine areas distributing his gourmet fare to hungry miners, long before he got to us. Plus, he rang a bell, and you could hear him even when he was miles away, thus paving the way for Mr Whippy way before his time.

Delightfully he could always be smelled and heard before he was seen, as he cooked them along the way in his wood oven. Dad would leave him a pile of wood from our mini sawmill to fire his oven, so without fail Mr. B very kindly threw in a couple of sausage rolls for us, and some scraps for the chickens or was it the other way around.

The "Dunnyman" was known for the same reasons as he drove his thirty-two-door sedan down the street to tidy up the toilet area; thankfully he never left us anything. I will break this little teaser down for the Gen Ys, bless their little hearts, and for the non-Aussies who may be more than curious as to who this man was, and what his purpose was.

I will just leave you with a brief outline. As we did not have Sewerage or Septic systems, or running water, a couple of dedicated guys drove an early version of a stretch Limo with several doors that held containers, some delivered and some taken away. Someone had to do it.

Progress has changed all of that for the better, but to be honest it did not do us any harm, in fact I believe it gave us the basics of putting systems together and placing them in the right order.

Things seem to have been less complicated back then. I somehow miss the simplicity and lack of drama because it was so much fun waiting in anticipation for a chat with delivery guys. They were like part of an extended family; we knew them by their first names.

Television arrived when I was a teenager, and it was in black and white. We did not care as it was such an added bonus to our monthly trip to the cinema on the train. This made life a little bit busier as we still had the newspaper delivered and we looked forward to reading the comics section. Not before the lord and master of the house had read it, that was the rule back then.

Looking back, I can see that progress was starting to gain a little momentum, but not enough to notice. It was happening at a slow pace and we grew into the changes comfortably. Sequences were becoming layers like rings in a tree.

— oOo —

However, in the last fifty to sixty years, that has all changed. The system has moved so fast, in fact there has never been a time in recorded history that so much happened in such a short-time.

Back to the milkman, before we speed off too far off into the future. He was the last of the delivery men as shops and malls sprang up around us. Even though we had moved to a bigger house on the property he still would deliver the milk and cream before sunrise and quite often our paths would cross. By this time, I was in my late teens and I was using up every second of a day living life and learning new skills. Alas, I lived on adrenalin and very little sleep.

More often than not I would be in a comatose state after a long day of rehearsals for the show that same night. Earlier the dressing room was a buzz as we did the whole stage makeup bit, then donned the costumes and waited in line with fifteen other dancers, then hit the spotlight as the curtain opened.

At this point my heartbeat was deafening as the adrenalin almost took my breath away and anxiety was at its peak until the music started. The second my ears heard the classical sounds from Swan Lake or the Sleeping Beauty, my trained body and mind automatically flowed in the rhythm.

Other times we would dance contemporary to "Putting on the Ritz", or a high kicking energetic dance to "New York, New York" or whatever fitted the theme of the Cabaret or stage show at the time. Ballroom dancing was part of my dance, sport and fitness life, and Latin Dance was my favourite. Ah the "Memories".

I would love to be able to move at the speed of sound like we did back then to quickly change to Waltz tempo and be totally lost in a gown that looked like a starched cloud, with your head poking out of the top. Not

——————— o0o ———————

to mention hanging on for dear life to a partner with a starched face poking out of a Tux.

In my early career as a fashion and theatrical costume designer, I travelled to most States with my fashion shows. I loved it with a passion as my greatest thrill was to get some local gals and guys that had not done much with their lives and show them how to use a catwalk. Teach them to dance, tart them up wearing some of my latest designs and let them rip.

I fondly remember our troupe bringing the house down in north Queensland with our rendition of "The Townsville Tapping Trollops" which was very risqué at that time to use that terminology, but it was tastefully done. The reward was fantastic to bring a sense of adventure to some country girls and guys of all ages who had never seen a sequin in their lives, let alone don some tap shoes and dance a catwalk in front of a live audience.

The milkman never saw the glamour of the spotlights; what he saw was the smudged mascara and very tired bags of feathers and sequins being dragged by a mere shell of a human stumbling through the door whilst tucking the bottles of milk under the arm as the shell waved goodbye.

Fortunately, what the lucky man did not see was the shower of sequins caught in the crosswinds head skywards and watch them in what seemed like slow motion as they slowly floated to the floor as I undressed and prepared for bed. At this point I caught sight of myself in the mirror and said, "Stuff it. I will clean this mess up in the morning."

So I hit the sack with gusto, which is not another dance move by the way. It means that all of my previous poise, glamour and discipline went down with the ship. Wait! That is not the end of the saga as morning brings on its own story of drama.

oOo

On one particular morning as I slowly attempted to move, one by one, each of my aching parts, it became apparent that I had survived through the night once again. I tried to prise open my eyes to have a look around and check to see if it was safe to breathe, because it is not uncommon to wake up with cracked ribs or sprained ankles or dislocated shoulders after a marathon.

This occasion I thought I had gone blind, as all I could see was darkness, so when the pins and needles slowly subsided from my left hand that I had been lying on for several hours, I reached up to inspect, to discover that the glue from my nine-inch eyelash had overheated and fused my eyelid to my cheek.

With that horrifying moment out of the way I thought it would be safe to get out of bed and attempt being vertical again. As I rolled onto my side, I saw a huge spider coming towards me, and my flight and fight response kicked in and I forgot about my bruised and battered body and leapt to my feet, only to come crashing back down as my leg went out from under me, due to the one, five-inch heel I still had on, and now as I was face to face with this formidable arachnoid. Reaching for the other five-inch heel dance shoe I beat the living daylights out of one of God's living creatures. The feelings of both remorse and conquest at the same time soon turned to humiliation as I discovered it was my other nine-inch eyelash.

That was a detour out of the way to get to my point of the importance of Sequences. In my world at the time of theatre, dance and fashion, I was surrounded by precision that involved feathers and sequins.

Dramatic gowns and costumes for the opera, stage productions, theatre, reviews, ballet, ballroom, singers, TV personalities; each garment had to depict a character and a story. To get the feel or the essence of a

———————————— o0o ————————————

production I would read the script with the producer and walk around the empty stage and picture what the character's role was in the story.

Each of the stories were so different, like The Mikado, The King and I, South Pacific, Oliver, Swan Lake, Sleeping Beauty and every Pantomime you can name. The bottom line is you have to start at the beginning with the end in mind.

With the end in mind, we have to work backwards to start with a plan, a purpose, an idea and a vision. Every stitch, sequin, and feather has to be put into a sequence for the right outcome and the best possible effect.

My outcome was seeing my creativity merge with like-minded talented people to burst into a production with stories and visual effects that bring entertainment that gives joy, moves emotions, and delivers pleasure.

My aim with this story is to point out the power of Strategy with Sequences. Little did I know way back then I was being groomed for a life with a purpose and it started with one sequin at a time, and just for the record I sewed on my first sequin when I was ten years old.

According to my Dick and Harry the definition of sequins are: usually round shiny metal discs that catch the light and make a garment shimmer. They like to stick together. Flash, gleam, glimmer, glint, glisten, shimmer, sparkle. These words mean "To send forth light".

The Venetians used gold coins for decorative purposes, old coins were used in Italy and Turkey to enhance a garment. The French had a go as far back as 1617. I suppose inflation put a stop to that.

A Sequence is: the order in which a group of related items is arranged. A successive order of things in a particular order in which related things follow one another. Connected or continuous things as in a subsequent event.

————————————————— oOo —————————————————

Special Sequence is when a sequence has a unique pattern to it. A combination of behavioural incidents directed towards a particular goal or outcome, as in getting ready for something.

-o0o-

Looking back at the patterns, strategies and sequences that somehow happened to shape my life, now seem to make sense. I did not set out with a plan with any successive order; little did I know that a combination of behavioural incidents would connect to outcomes that I experience today.

It is crystal clear that my identity and image were being fulfilled in sequences along the way from the dreams and desires that never wavered since I was a pigtailed introverted kid from the bush. I can still see the white leather-bound Encyclopedia Britannica Volume One on the shelf in the bookcase, beckoning me to open the pages to stare and dream longingly at Dame Margot Fonteyn, ballerina extraordinaire.

I never had a hope of reaching her brilliance, but the fire in my belly made sure every dancer I worked with looked and felt like her. I can't even describe the feeling of the euphoric satisfaction of just starting with a dream, a vision that was being created one stitch and sequin at a time.

Volume Two was just as alluring to me; it held images of far-off places yet to be explored. I remember running my hand down the pages across the photos of London, Paris, Budapest, Hong Kong, New York and more, picturing myself walking through the streets and gardens of what to me was so exotic at the time.

Imagination is the core of creativity and creativity is the core of imagination. If you download the images in your mind, your creativity automatically brings the images into reality.

o0o

Never did I dream way back then that I would make a career out of visiting those very places, by taking photographs, writing about how wonderful it is to visit the towns and cities and interviewing the local people.

I had all of the above, which was wonderful and very rewarding in many ways, but what I did not have was a SYSTEM to monetise the many sequences and strategies that I had experienced. By creating a system, it creates good habits and builds the big wheel that drives all of the little wheels that make movement happen.

By placing that system wheel in front of all of your talents dreams, will move your life organically and automatically leaving no room for doubt.

> 66
>
> *Power of Habits "People do not decide their future, they decide their habits and their habits decide their future."*
>
> - F. Matthais Alexander

Final thoughts…

> 66
>
> *"Experience is something you don't get until just after you need it"*
>
> - Steven Wright

www.MaeRoseMethods.com

I have enjoyed sharing this book with you. I do hope you can relate to some of the comments and experiences and you've had a laugh or a tear or two along the way. Mostly I am sincerely anticipating that I have inspired and excited you to live with intent and prosper for the rest of your life.

I'm proud to have the privilege of putting together the first edition of this revolutionary anti-aging "owner's manual" for successful sizzling seniors, and I am sure it will help you stay active, attractive, and young at heart. You've got nothing to lose by trying it…. except your wrinkles, and an empty bank account.

My intent with this book is to pay homage to all seniors who have added so much grace to our lives with their presence, uniqueness, wisdom and experience. Their unwavering spirit, resilience and perseverance are a testament to the power of aging gracefully.

Cherish the present moments in the relationships we have with our loved ones, find joy in the simplest of things. Highly value the complex moments and events as they put magic in the mystery.

This is the beginning of many valuable and abundant lessons on how you can make a change, regardless of age or status. It is the stories you make and experiences that will help and shape our lives and the lives of our younger generations to come.

Through dedicated guidance and mentorship my team and I are eager to assist you to navigate life's challenges and overcome any obstacles and remove the negativity of learned behaviour that does not serve us.

I have written this book as a celebration of my life and the teachings I have received. It is a reminder of the benefits of growing older, the richness that comes with each experience, and the wisdom that only time can bring.

—————————————————— o0o ——————————————————

Ridding ourselves of limiting beliefs and myths about aging separates the facts from fiction and fills in the gaps so we can live younger, longer. Any of us, indeed most of us, can slow down or reverse the effects of aging. Change the belief that aging is not the normal and natural consequence that we will all suffer like it is a disease.

Showing how the process can be slowed and halted is my passion. Sharing the science of aging is why I am an ambassador of "Living Younger Longer", hence the creation of Mae-Rose Essentials Products which are practical tools that you can apply in your everyday life.

As we age, we may start to develop a sense of acceptance about the myths of aging that can hinder our ability to outsmart the declining cells. These beliefs and habits can be damaging to our mental, physical and emotional well-being, and can prevent us from reaching our full potential.

Let's recap below some of the most common beliefs and myths about aging and provide tips on how to separate fact from fiction.

Myth #1: Aging means declining health and mobility. While it is true that our bodies change as we age, and we may experience some physical limitations, it is not inevitable that we become weaker or find it harder to move. In fact, there are many ways to maintain and even improve our health and mobility as we age. Realistic and regular exercise, a sensible healthy eating regime and staying socially active are just a few examples of ways to outsmart the clock.

Myth #2: Older people can't learn new things, which is another common piece of brainwashing. This belief is not only false but damaging to our emotional and mental state. Learning new things has been scientifically proven to keep our brains active and stimulated. Keeping engaged can even prevent cognitive decline. It is never too late to learn something new, like learning a new language or mastering a new skill.

o0o

Myth #3: The belief of many people is that aging means becoming isolated and lonely, but that does not have to be the case. Push back at that worn out excuse and become more socially involved with clubs, groups or charities. Volunteering will not only help you but can help combat isolation and loneliness in others. Stay in touch with friends and family, command the preservation of family unions, which is the case in more tribal societies. Use our wisdom and retrain society about the value of the elders.

Myth #4: Older people are not interested in technology, which is another myth about aging. While it is true that some older people may not be as familiar with the latest gadgets and apps, many are eager to learn and stay connected through technology. In fact, I know several people who stay connected using their own iPad and mobile phones. They are so grateful that they can actually communicate face to face with friends and family, something that was unheard of when we were young. We are all so appreciative that we live in an age where we can learn new things. I believe it definitely improves our health on so many levels.

Myth #5: Many people believe that aging means losing your independence. While it is true that some older adults may require assistance with daily activities, it is more than possible to maintain our independence and autonomy. With the help of assistive devices, home modifications, and supportive services, many older adults are able to live independently for many years. In fact, many of the people I interviewed live were online via Zoom. Some were on Facetime on their phones. Some sent stories by email and text.

I asked them how they acquired the knowledge of how to use technology, their unanimous and delightful replies were varied and interesting. Mostly some were assisted by patient and understanding family members, others hired a coach or went to lessons, love the smug answers from a few rebels who stated with a glint in their eye "I taught myself".

—————————————— oOo ——————————————

What was most fascinating is a lot of them were still proficient using Shorthand writing which is an abbreviated symbolic writing method that increases the speed at which you write. It is also called speed or narrow writing The purpose is to be able to write approximately as fast as someone speaks, in order to take down everything that is said. In my early career, I worked in Pharmacies, where we wrote a lot of terms in Latin, plus most dictation were done in shorthand.

When doing my research, I found a few old girls like me still using both forms of writing, so just for old times' sake we had a laugh by writing our shopping lists then seeing if we could translate each other's lists. Ask your Nan, she may still dabble in a little sneaky narrow writing (shorthand writing) when she wants to write something she does not want you to read.

I stood and cheered and applauded when I learned that "Morse Code" is something they can still read and hear because it was handed down from family members who were military trained. They were interested enough to keep it alive so not to lose that part of history. I still have the little machine my father gave to me, along with the written material on how to use the codes.

If this subject interests you do some research.

Google quote: International Morse Code was used in World War II and the Korean and Vietnam wars. It was used heavily by the shipping industry and for the safety of the seas up until the early 1990's.

Little do the younger ones (the people who insist that we are too old) know that they do not have any idea that they are being outsmarted by an old form of technology. I defy any one of them to master that incredible form of communication. So stick that in your left ventricle doubting Thomas and Co.

—————————————————— o0o ——————————————————

It's important to separate fact and fiction like the above story when it comes to aging. Limiting beliefs and harmful myths about aging can prevent us from living our best lives. Stand up and push back at this worn out set of controlling assumptions that have whiskers on them by staying active, engaged and informed, so we can age backwards and continue to live younger longer. So let's embrace the opportunities that come with a few years under our belt, and live with conviction and purpose, no matter what our age.

Being educated on how to learn and grow rich is not a mystery if we remove the blockages and fear of obtaining great wealth. Many people have a fear of wealth success, and that learned fear can prevent us from reaching our full financial potential. Often, this is rooted in limiting beliefs and blockages that are really difficult to overcome.

We have issued a serve of strategies to explore how easy it is to apply a system for removing obstacles based on fear and ignorance.

Step 1: The first step in removing blockages and fear of obtaining great wealth is to identify and address your limiting beliefs. These beliefs can be deeply ingrained and can hold you back from achieving your full potential. For example, you may believe that money is evil or that wealthy people are greedy. These beliefs may have been instilled into your psyche when you were a child; this in turn can give you a feeling of guilt and possible shame, preventing you from taking the necessary steps to grow your wealth.

To overcome these harmful beliefs, start by questioning their validity, ask yourself where these ideas came from and whether they are based on facts or assumptions. Then reframe your beliefs in a more positive way. For example, instead of believing that money is evil, you can also reprogram your mind to know that money is a valuable tool.

———————————— o0o ————————————

Step 2: Once you have addressed your limiting beliefs, and you have a healthy attitude toward earning what you are worth, it's time to set clear financial goals. Without clarity it can be difficult to know where to focus your energy resources. When setting and targeting your goals, be specific and realistic. If you want to increase your income, set a precise dollar amount that you want to earn each year.

Step 3: With clear financial goals in place, it's time to develop a plan or a strategy to achieve them. This plan should include specific actions that will enable you to grow your wealth, such as investing in stocks or real estate, starting a business, or developing a new skill set. Break your plan down into accurate smaller and manageable steps that you can work comfortably with on a daily or weekly basis.

Step 4: In order to learn and grow rich, you must be willing to invest in yourself. This means continually learning new skills and expanding your knowledge. Attend seminars, read books, seek out mentors who can help you achieve and reach your goals and dreams. By investing in yourself, you will be better equipped to make informed decisions and take calculated risks that can lead to greater wealth and success.

Removing blockages and the fear of obtaining great wealth from your skills and experience requires a combination of self-reflection, goal-setting, planning and continuous learning. By taking these positive steps, you can overcome your limitations and take action toward achieving your financial goals. So, embrace the opportunities that come with growing your wealth and knowledge, and use your skills and experience to learn and grow rich.

66

"Invest in yourself despite the opinion of others."

- Mae-Rose

oOo

Below are some of the many things that my team and I can support you with under our general marketing and mentoring program by creating a System, a Strategy to line up with Sequences for your guaranteed Success: MaeDaze Million Dollar Marketing:

* How to become attitude ambassadors, think prosperity, passion, preparation and purpose for success.

* Learn how rewarding it is to learn new skills without having to have a degree or formal education.

* Choose from the abundance of opportunities available for seniors just from Google alone without any risks.

* We can teach how to start small and grow huge by making available the multiple streams of income that you can do from home or on holidays.

* You will gain confidence knowing why seniors are better in business.

* Not to be afraid as you don't have to do it on your own. We have a step-by-step Seniors Wealth Map to follow in sequences to learn the truth about being wealthy.

* We can teach you the do's and don'ts to maintain a healthy body and mind for practical and senior health and well-being without having to go to a gym to perform unrealistic strenuous routines.

* We will show you how to travel in style and comfort and enjoy every minute without being tired and drained.

* Having a sense of humour, laughing and having fun is the best medicine. To embrace the funny side of life and aging.

* We will show you how to start a small profitable business or hobby.

———————————————— o0o ————————————————

If you choose to write a book, we can guide you in the right direction to the best publishers in the world.

* Having a virtual assistant to do most of the work allows you to work on your projects and not work up to your neck in the protocols, saving hours of stress and worry.

* If you want a big or bigger business or career, we can instruct you on the importance of having your own personal brand that will escalate your success.

* Show you how to travel first class wherever you go and avoid the pitfalls mentioned in Chapter Seven.

* We show you how to safeguard your assets by gaining high-end financial guidance and advice from experts. How to manage your finances and avoid the traps.

Wealth in all its shapes and forms is a flowing river, it has to circulate, it must spread and flow, and cascade. It is an incredible servant, and the truth is there is abundance of all things, so attain all you can, save and nurture all you can, give all you can.

Learn from the years of experience and training from Team Mae-Rose, who are dedicated to helping you achieve your success. We have come up with a solid team and experience through thorough mentorship and training. We are happy to share our knowledge, wisdom and expertise with all of you so you may be the next, head turning example of holding on strong and shining. Become part of our revolutionary quest to become the largest group of sizzling *"Successful Seniors"* in all of history.

With gratitude, admiration, passion and purpose…

I am sincerely yours,

Mae-Rose

———————————————— oOo ————————————————

"

"Invest In yourself to get the best interest"

- Debasish Mridha

GET On STRONG...Hold ON

www.MaeRoseMethods.com

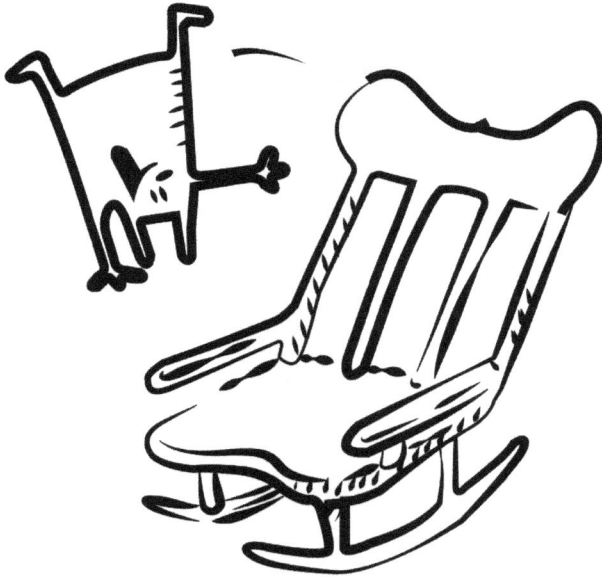

FREE BONUS OFFERS, JUST FOR PURCHASING THIS BOOK

You are now witnessing a world of opportunity, where you can unlock your full potential and achieve success in both your personal and professional life. We are excited to offer you a range of complimentary resources that are designed to help you maximise your potential and take your life and business to the next level.

Bonus Chapter

You can obtain and additional chapter, the bonus chapter to this book, where I share with you the culmination of all my efforts in achieving success in various aspects of life. In this chapter, you will witness the completion of my projects, the culmination of my literary endeavours, and the attainment of optimal health and wealth. I am thrilled to share this journey with you and hope that you will find inspiration and motivation in my story. So sit back, relax, and enjoy reading as I take you through my personal triumphs and victories.

To receive this Free Gift, simply send an email to endresults1@gmail.com with Free Bonus in the subject line and we will get this and the other free gifts to you.

---------------- o0o ----------------

FREE 30 MIN Consultation with the Branding Queen - Mae-Rose

Are you struggling with establishing your brand and developing an effective marketing strategy? Look no further, as we offer you a complimentary 30 minute consultation with Mae-Rose, the renowned branding queen. Mae-Rose is an expert in branding and marketing and has helped numerous clients establish their brand and increase their revenue. Book your free consultation today and discover how Mae-Rose can help you reach your branding and marketing goals.

If you haven't done so already, simply email endresults1@gmail.com with Free Bonus in the subject line to receive this and other gifts all FREE.

FREE Access to Strategic Life Online Course - Tips on how to be strategic and be successful in life and business

Do you want to learn how to be more strategic and successful in life and business? We are pleased to offer you free access to our Strategic Life Online Course which offers a range of valuable tips and strategies that will help you achieve success in all aspects of your life. The course covers a variety of topics, including goal setting, time management, and effective communication, among others. Enrol now and start your journey towards success.

Email endresults1@gmail.com with Free Bonus in the subject line.

oOo

Complimentary Ticket to our Webinar on Wealth Building & Marketing

Do you want to learn more about wealth building and marketing? We are excited to offer you a complimentary ticket to our upcoming webinar, where you will hear from industry experts on business strategy, social media, and branding. Our speakers are highly experienced professionals who will provide valuable insights and tips to help you grow your business and increase your revenue. Simply email us at endresults1@gmail.com to register and secure your spot today and obtain all the bonuses listed here, completely FREE.

The Seniors Wealth Map

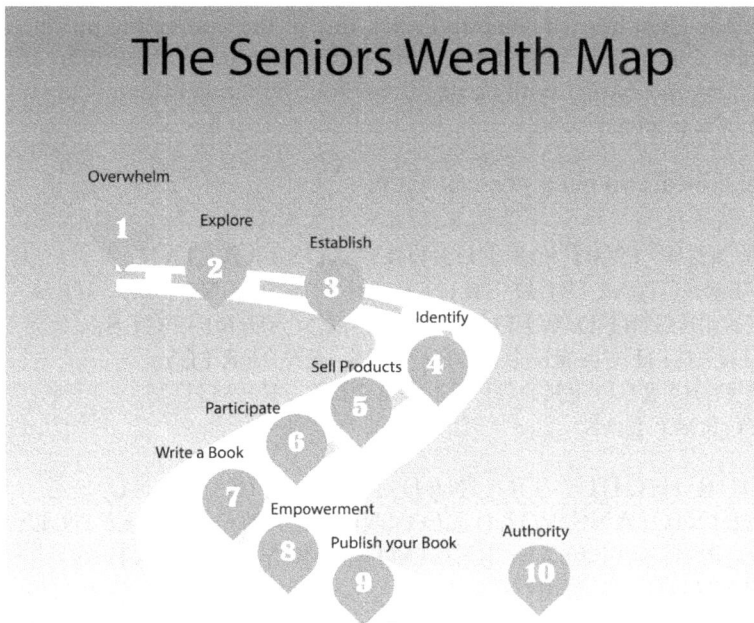

oOo

Mae-Rose Essentials

We've found an entirely new type of skin care range. One that nourishes your skin from its deepest cells and could change the way you care for your skin forever.

Made right here in Australia, each one of these amazing products can completely transform your skin, leaving it healthier and younger looking, with no negative environmental effects – to you, or the planet.

A skincare so pure, you can eat it.

A NEW TYPE OF LUXURY AUSTRALIAN PERSONALISED SKIN CARE, ESSENTIAL OILS ENERGISED WITH CRYSTALS, PERFUMES, HEALTH CARE PRODUCTS, EXPERTLY PREPARED PRODUCTS WITH PREMIUM FORMULAS.

OUR HIGHLY TRAINED THERAPISTS AND CLINICIANS WILL LOVINGLY AND CAREFULLY PERSONALISE A REGIME FOR YOU THAT IS UNIQUELY YOURS!!!

www.MaeRoseEssentials.com

oOo

Questionnaire

NAME:

EMAIL:

ADDRESS:

Fill out the questionnaire below and discover your Ayurvedic Element which may be either Fire, Water, Air, or Earth. This is a fun and informative exercise that will give you a better understanding of yourself, especially when you come to read my next book!

For each question, place a tick in the box next to the trait that best describes you in general. When completed, scan or photograph it and email it to endresults1@gmail.com and I will reply with the insights.

Which of the following describes you?

☐ Active/Energetic

☐ Patient

☐ Sensitive

☐ Intellectual

What colours do you like to wear?

☐ Earthy/Rustic

☐ Bright/Vibrant

☐ Flamboyant

☐ Subtle

————— o0o —————

What clothes make you feel comfortable?

☐ Flowing

☐ Colourful

☐ Fashionable

☐ Practical

Most happy when in the company of people who give you?

☐ Security

☐ Prestige

☐ Recognition

☐ Appreciation

What type of food taste do you prefer?

☐ Sour

☐ Hot

☐ Salty

☐ Sweet

If you have a slight car accident, do you:

☐ Take their details

☐ Discuss the incident

☐ Get angry at the other driver

☐ Check if anyone is hurt

When someone suggests a restaurant you often eat at, do you say:

☐ "It's not very good" as you would rather go somewhere else

——————————————— o0o ———————————————

☐ "That will be fine"

☐ "I've dined here before" and wait for their response

☐ Offer to dine at your place

When choosing clothes, are your decisions:

☐ Made quickly

☐ Based on value

☐ Guided by trends

☐ Just love the fabric

The people you are drawn to:

☐ Calculate risks

☐ Prefer facts

☐ Quick decision makers

☐ Solid in their procedure

Having a down day, do you feel:

☐ Unsociable, tired, on edge

☐ Tearful, sensitive vulnerable

☐ Stuck, bored, worried

☐ Overwhelmed, irritable, burnt out

When you feel good and in control, you are:

- ☐ Stable, reliable, balanced
- ☐ Creative, thoughtful, in touch with emotions
- ☐ Energetic, full of life, optimistic
- ☐ Sociable, expressive, open

Participating in a group in an activity, do you:

- ☐ Prefer to lead
- ☐ Want things to run smoothly and happily
- ☐ Generate ideas
- ☐ Carry out allocated tasks effectively

OTHER RECOMMENDED RESOURCES

MaeDaze Million $ Marketing	www.mdmilliondollarmarketing.com
Global Publishing Group	www.GlobalPublishingGroup.com.au
Peter McLaughlin Red Chip Lawyers	www.RedChip.com.au
https://livegoodtour.com/maerose	

www.MaeRoseMethods.com

ABOUT THE AUTHOR

Mae-Rose O'Connell is an international author, educator, speaker and natural health and wellness therapist.

Her zest for life comes from her background in physical fitness and dance, and she has qualifications in modern gymnastics, aerobics, yoga and dance sport.

She is the founder and director of the End Results Academy, an organisation that is dedicated to providing workshops, seminars, training and coaching in lifestyle, fitness, health, nutrition, wealth and technology. It has been operating since 1983.

Interviewing, speaking, coaching, and writing about natural health and ageing well are Mae-Rose's professional passions. This quote from her perfectly captures the natural health philosophy that she likes to inspire in others: "Be a transmitter of health, wealth, and knowledge."

Mae-Rose has been practising both natural and alternative health therapies for more than 35 years, including iridology, mineral therapy, reflexology, myofascial release, Swedish massage, polarity therapy, Ayurvedic marma points therapy, detoxing, Gestalt psychology and

————————— o0o —————————

colon hydrotherapy. In addition, she facilitates creative self-image, voice dialogue, and body language coaching.

Mae-Rose has a Diploma in Fashion and Costume Design and utilises her knowledge in this area to coach her clients in the importance of dressing for success and showing how colour and style has a major impact on branding. The psychology of knowing what looks good and the impact this has on your self-esteem and attitude is what Mae-Rose is passionate about helping others to radiate!

In her spare time, Mae-Rose loves to travel, write, and photograph both places and people that interest her. "If life is a journey and death is inevitable, then I am going via the scenic route," she says.

Mae-Rose also has an insatiable desire for adventure. She has travelled extensively both throughout Australia and internationally, having visited 27 countries. She maintains that the highlight of her life's travels has been her journey of self-discovery.

Mae-Rose now lives on the Gold Coast in Queensland, Australia.

—————————————— oOo ——————————————

www.ingramcontent.com/pod-product-compliance
Lightning Source LLC
Chambersburg PA
CBHW072149090426
42740CB00012B/2200